# #BreakInto VC

## HOW TO BREAK INTO
## VENTURE CAPITAL

And Think Like an Investor Whether You're a
Student, Entrepreneur or Working Professional

BRADLEY MILES

Published by Bradley Miles
ISBN 978-1-5449343-4-1

Copyright © Bradley Miles, 2017

Visit Bradley Miles' official website at www.breakintovc.com
for the latest news, book details, and other information.

Book layout by Guido Henkel

Use the hashtag *#BreakIntoVC*
when discussing this book on social media!

We regularly release new interviews, articles and posts,
all to help people break into VC.

Join our e-mail list at *breakintovc.com*

*To: Mary W. and Christopher W.*

"Breaking into VC is perhaps one of the hardest challenges in the business world unless you happen to be Bradley Miles. This young VC/author developed relationships and expertise in the industry by building a blog following and doing original research on bitcoin and blockchain. Bradley was fearless in reaching out to industry veterans and showed genuine interest in and knowledge of their work. To those with similar heart, intellect and grit, Bradley shines a light on the mysterious and arcane world of venture."
**— Miriam Rivera, Partner at Ulu Ventures**

"*#BreakIntoVC* is the most detailed and informative resource out there for anyone wanting to learn more about venture capital. Bradley comprehensively demystifies the industry and I would recommend this as a must-read for anyone interested in the intersection between entrepreneurship and finance."
**— George Liu, Partner at Dorm Room Fund**

"A practical guide that decodes the language needed to understand the VC world. The hustle is not included, but if you are picking this book up that's a good sign."
**— Aaron Walker, Founder at Camelback Ventures**

# INTRODUCTION

I never came across a simple and thoughtful guide that walks regular people through the investor mindset.

I found a lot of this knowledge hidden in conversations with friends after I became a venture capitalist or locked inside the ivory towers of elite institutions.

I've always thought that it's regular people who start great businesses and regular people who become the most sought after venture capitalists.

Since many agree that there is no better time to start a business than right now, thinking like an investor has become crucial to success in the modern age.

But the journey starts with being able to answer simple questions like, "What is venture capital?" and learning how to pitch a company successfully in order to land meetings and interviews.

Have you ever thought of being on the other side of the table when it came to investing?

What's it like to be the person that everyone is chasing down to invest in their company?

#BreakIntoVC teaches you how to think like an investor and helps you thrive whether your goal is to break into the incredible field of venture capital or fund that startup idea you've been thinking of for months, maybe even years.

This book is for people who want to know a little more about the intricate and opaque world of venture investing, but never found a simple and approachable guide that sums it all up in one easy to read book.

I wrote *#BreakIntoVC* as a guide for you because getting into venture capital was tough for me. I didn't have all those fancy friends that endorsed the book when I first started. I didn't have anyone, really. I was scrounging through the internet, scraping articles and blog posts from across the web and trying to work these ideas into strong pitches that would impress investors.

Eventually, I came up with a blueprint to learn how to talk to VCs and land an offer at a top venture capital firm. This book is that blueprint.

I'll teach you about the different types of investors out there and why every venture capitalist doesn't invest in every deal. Put your dusty old 400-page accounting textbook back on the shelf, I'll guide you through all the accounting and finance you'll ever need to know in order to understand the industry and really start thinking like an investor.

By the end of this book you'll know how to talk about companies that excite you, pitch companies to venture capitalists and evaluate businesses through the lens of an investor.

Whether you're looking to enter the venture capital industry or start a business, the real gift of this book is gaining the mindset of a venture capitalist and being able to understand markets and companies so well that you can win over investors again and again in meetings and pitches.

I've since tested the strategies in this helpful how-to guide with dozens of folks across the country. In between finishing the manuscript and publishing *#BreakIntoVC*, I gave the book to several of my friends in the industry, who then passed it on to their friends.

The result was meeting people like Arjun, a working professional who was coming across the same old problems that I faced: too many terms and concepts scattered across the web with little or no guidance. After reading *#BreakIntoVC*, Arjun was easily able to identify and address any gaps in knowledge before sitting down to speak with investors.

I got to know Nicholas, who dreams of getting funding for his video streaming startup so he can take the independent music world by storm. After reading an advanced copy of #BreakIntoVC and a short conversation, Nicholas now truly understands his market and came up with a killer strategy to expand his platform and become a signal above all the noise.

I met folks like John, a student who was eager to get into venture capital, but needed to really understand the mechanics of how to pitch a company before asking a few friends for an introduction to investors. John now has two pitches ready to go in diverse sectors that really show off his expertise and ability to think like a VC.

I became close with Mac, a student who attends a "non-core" school where venture capital firms do not necessarily recruit. After reading Chapter 16, a guide to starting a venture club on your college campus, Mac is quickly becoming one of the go-to students on campus for venture capital-related events and project-based learning opportunities with investors.

After speaking with entrepreneurs looking for funding, working professionals in tech, banking or consulting, and students from USC, Wharton, Manhattan College, Stanford, Harvard, University of Colorado Boulder, USC and many others, I can assure you that the techniques in this book work.

I promise that if you follow the techniques and strategies I outline in this book, you'll have everything you need to win over the hearts and minds of even the most hard to reach investors tucked away in the hills of Silicon Valley.

For the entrepreneurs out there: venture capitalists invest in people. Once you understand how to pitch a company, even if investors think your idea isn't a home run, they'll be confident enough in you to offer some advice and you can continue to build a relationship that could last a lifetime. All from a successful pitch.

Regardless of whether your goal is to become a venture capitalist or get your company funded, you need to learn how to think and communicate like an investor. This is the quickest way to thrive as you begin your journey.

Don't be the person who sits at home watching Shark Tank, secretly wishing for a seat at the investor table. The longer you sit on the sidelines, the harder it is to get in the game.

Be the proactive person who's tackling industries and really making an effort to understand the ever changing tech sector. Put on the helmet and be the type of person who takes action and does so immediately.

The tips and tricks I'm about to show you get results. I'll take you by the hand with each chapter and show you the best way to reach out to tech folks and investors in your community, walk you through case study pitches, valuation methods, mock calls and even introduce you to some folks who did it an entirely different way. All you need to do is keep reading.

Let's put in the work together and head towards the new life you're about to create.

What are you waiting for? Let's break in!

# Chapter 1
# CONVENTIONAL WISDOM

Barclays Capital is located in the old Lehman Brothers building adjacent to Times Square. From the main cafeteria, you can see all the lights and skyscrapers the city has to offer. I learned a lot at Barclays during the summer of my sophomore year. I learned how to model financial data, be efficient in Microsoft Excel and work from 8:50am to 4:00am. However, and most importantly, I learned I did not want to do banking.

To me, the experience of spending a summer in investment banking was like having 30 days left to live. Investment banking swallows an enormous amount of your day. So much so, that you start to realize what actually matters to you. It's almost as if you are developing a mental bucket list of the things you wish you could do, but simply don't have the *bandwidth* to do.

After several nights of pacing around that cafeteria after midnight, the artificial lights and billboards of the city started to look alien. The surrounding darkness began to recall some strange space oddity as if Gene Roddenberry and Jordan Belfort were locked in a room, had drunk way too much alcohol and then decided to write a television pilot together.

I started to feel trapped, especially after being told, "Hey, you need to do two years of this first before VC" or "Hey, you need to do two years of consulting first," and I just did not want to go that route. I wanted the adrenaline rush of working with founders and touching the entrepreneurial process again.

What really mattered to me in that weird investment banking spaceship moment was pursuing venture capital and doing it right now—while a student, even if the odds were stacked against me and even if I wasn't aware of anyone who had actually accomplished this before.

It was in that moment I decided to hop off the ship, and try to break into venture capital.

Breaking into venture capital can be challenging, but it is doable. I want to share some conventional wisdom that was passed along to me when I first realized a career in venture capital was right for me.

> Person A: *Well, you need to work in the Technology or TMT sector of a top-notch bulge bracket investment bank for two years. After your two-year stint, recruiters will place you in a late stage venture capital firm.*

> Person B: *I worked in management consulting for two years with a focus on the technology sector. I networked with venture capitalists during my off-hours and landed a few interviews in my last year as a consultant.*

> Person C: *I spent four years after undergrad working in finance and after getting my MBA from [Top 15 Business School], I was able to land several interviews in the industry.*

These are all viable ways to break into venture capital but I want to do away with the myth that these are the *only* ways to do so. After speaking with the people above in my early years of undergrad, I decided the best course of action for me, was to pursue an internship in investment banking, strive for and get a full-time offer and work for two years in order to break into venture capital.

I studied behavioral questions, valuation techniques, *Wall Street Oasis* and *Mergers & Inquisitions* guides endlessly. I landed an internship at a top investment bank in the tech sector. I was finally on what I envisioned to be the right path, and I was miserable.

I played along for 10 weeks but in my heart, I knew the 120+ hour work lifestyle was not something I could benefit from in the long-term. As the internship continued, I also realized *why* I wanted to work in venture capital so much. It was the adrenaline rush of being in front of entrepreneurs and working with them each and every day. The feeling that a venture capital job wouldn't even really feel like work because I was so enthralled with the process of helping young companies grow.

Chapter 2
# EARLY STAGE INVESTING
*AN OVERVIEW OF THE INDUSTRY*

## What Is Venture Capital?

Let's say you and I decided to start a gluten-free grocery delivery service. We would likely need the support and financial resources of investors with domain expertise in our field to become successful.

If those investors received their money from several different sources who did not directly own a percentage of the portfolio companies, then those individuals are *venture capitalists* and they are receiving money from *limited partners* (these are endowments, foundations, public pensions, high net worth individuals etc.). In chapter 14, I will dive into what precisely makes a venture-backable business.

In this case, we can call venture capital the money we are receiving in order to grow our early stage business. When I use the term early stage, I am referring to both private businesses at ground zero, as well as mid-level private businesses that need assistance in order to reach further milestones.

The venture capital industry invests in businesses like our little 'startup that could'—companies with huge risk and little-to-no proven track record—as well as growing businesses like Uber and Seamless that need help in any number of areas like continued branding or international expansion.

## How Does It Work?

Cynthia and Mercedes get together and want to start a venture capital firm, but first they need money to invest. They pitch the idea of their fund to a college endowment as well as a public pension fund.

The endowment and pension fund agree to invest. Cynthia and Mercedes then form "CynMerc" Ventures, which will invest in early stage private companies. With this first fund—let's call it CynMerc I, CynMerc Ventures will spend 3-5 years investing the money and 5 more years (8 to 10 years in total) to get the pension and endowment money back plus a sufficient return on the investment to appease the endowment and pension fund.

Throughout the life of CynMerc I, Cynthia and Mercedes will look for markets and opportunities with substantial returns. They will try to invest as early as they can for a larger share of the company at a lesser cost, and may continue to invest through future funds (CynMerc II) so their share in the investment—or their *equity* stake, does not reduce in ownership, or *dilute* over time. CynMerc II will come in when about 75 percent of CynMerc I is committed to deals, this way CynMerc Ventures will always carry a substantial amount of capital in its coffers.

Cynthia and Mercedes will likely raise CynMerc II about 5-7 years into the life cycle of CynMerc I so the company never reaches a point where they have no more *committed capital*—or cash received from LPs—whenever an investment decision is reached by the firm for follow-on investments. The average fund size of all venture capital stages is about $400M and the average venture capital deal size is $18M.[1]

The larger the firm's stake in the company as shown in the account of all major shareholders, or *capitalization table*, the larger CynMerc's returns are when the company makes an exit either through an *initial public offering (IPO)* or any *mergers & acquisitions (M&A)* activity.

Since Cynthia and Mercedes are partners at CynMerc, they will charge a management fee of about 2 percent to the limited partners in order to pay their own salaries, and the salaries of the associates and the support staff (you).

Once the limited partners receive 100 percent of their money back, Cynthia and Mercedes receive 20 percent of any additional profits while the limited partners receive 80 percent. The 20 percent that Cynthia and Mercedes receive is referred to as *carried interest*.

## Venture Capital and Angel Investing

You will notice throughout the book that I use the term venture capital quite loosely. This reflects how the term is used in the industry as well. However, there is a structural difference between venture capital and angel investing, and I'd like to clear this up before moving forward.

Angel investors are individuals investing their own money. If Mercedes struck out on her own and left CynMerc Ventures, she would be considered an angel investor if she continued to invest in early stage companies. The big difference here is angels invest their own money while venture capitalists primarily invest other people's money. Traditionally, angel investors are also one of the earliest investors, often before a sellable product exists (hence, "angel").

## Why People Invest in Venture Capital

Despite such a high risk, limited partners agree to invest in venture firms in order to diversify their *assets*, or what they own. Instead of allocating capital only to stocks, bonds and real estate, portfolio managers allocate a portion of funds to a category known as *alternative investments*, which consists of private equity and venture capital investment opportunities. Since VC is so risky, usually under 15 percent of the portfolio is allocated to alternative investments.

For instance, VC firms return 25 percent on average, while the typical stock market return in a given year is 8 percent annually. That being said, it is rare for stocks to hit 0 dollars in value while in any given early stage portfolio over half of the companies may fail in a 10-year period. As usual, great returns come with great risk.

## Where You Come in

This book isn't about Cynthia or Mercedes. It's about you and your journey to break into venture capital. You are the support staff that will help Cynthia and Mercedes find incredible companies at an early stage in their lifecycle.

## Becoming an Entrepreneur vs. VC

All you need at this stage is an intellectual curiosity to learn more about technology markets and companies. If you've ever thought about starting a company, and it's not a burning desire that keeps you up through the night, you're probably not ready to drop everything and become an entrepreneur.

Spending a year or two in venture may be the next best thing. It will allow you to understand what makes a viable business in the long term, and how technology markets actually function. For example, if you want to start a drone business but you're not quite ready, talking to the CEO of a rapidly growing drone business is likely the next best thing.

Each conversation you have with an entrepreneur will feel like a class. If you talk to an entrepreneur who has five years of drone experience, you'll come out of the meeting not only knowing about their businesses in particular, but the drone market in general. You'll also gain an understanding in Healthcare IT, Branded Consumer Products and Internet software, marketplaces, govtech (government technology), edtech (education technology) and whichever other sectors your firm operates. After a few months, you may even find yourself consumed by an entire different industry. Imagine how expansive your knowledge set will be after two years. Let's get started!

# Chapter 3
# EARLY STEPS: REACHING OUT
*RESEARCH ENTREPRENEURS IN YOUR AREA*

It doesn't matter, but it helps, if you attend or previously attended an undergraduate business school or well-known university. If you are building relationships with the entrepreneurs in your area, you are on your way to landing your first venture capital opportunity.

Whether you go to school in a major city (SF, Boston, NYC, Chicago, Atlanta) or even a smaller city, you can still find venture capital opportunities.

The first step is to speak with an entrepreneur in your area, someone who has founded a startup and has been through at least an initial funding, or *seed round*. Most of the time, entrepreneurs and founders are genuinely friendly people and will hop on the phone with you for a 15-minute call or share some of their wisdom through e-mail.

To prove my point, go read the Hubspot Culture Code. Hubspot is a publicly traded company that creates inbound marketing software and was founded by Dharmesh Shah and Brian Halligan in Boston. Send an e-mail to the founder's address at the end of the slide and see how long it takes him to reply.

If you have Twitter (and you should) you can generally reach out to an entrepreneur by @ replying, "hey, do you have an e-mail I can send a quick note to?" LinkedIn is also a decent way of connecting with entrepreneurs. If you're having trouble finding entrepreneurs in your area, search your city on AngelList.

Alternatively, there are applications that allow you to guess or "hack" the e-mail address of an individual. Since most startup founders have a FirstName@startup.com or FirstInitialLastName@startup.com address, certain software can then trace this e-mail address back to their

LinkedIn while other programs can scrape through web searches to find the precise company e-mail format.

Now that we have an e-mail address of the entrepreneur, what do we say?

First you need a great subject line. Something short and striking like "I Need Your Help" or "Advice" will work fine. Next, draft a short e-mail that won't take too much time to read:

> My name is _____, I go to (school) and study (subject). Congratulations on (relevant startup event), I am excited to see how this progresses.
>
> I feel I have a genuine interest in early stage companies and would love to get some advice on navigating the startup ecosystem in_____.

Tweak this format to fit your needs, but the important thing is to show genuine interest in their company and ask for advice.

Speak with at least three entrepreneurs in your local area over the phone and ask:

> Can I learn a little more about your journey to become a funded company?
>
> What was the single greatest resource that you used as an entrepreneur to help you get funding?
>
> What other companies should I be aware of in _____?
>
> What do you think the future climate will be for startups in _____? Will there be less funding?
>
> Working in the venture space is a real passion of mine, I'd love to work with startups like yours in the future. Do you know anyone at (venture capital firm) who would be interested in speaking with me?

If the entrepreneur offers to send an introduction, try and follow 42Floors' e-mail introduction etiquette post where they suggest sending a new 1-2 paragraph e-mail about yourself to the founder that they can easily forward to the VC without exposing the previous conversation.

Chapter 4
# EARLY STEPS: OVERALL RESEARCH
*DEVELOP A PERSPECTIVE ON VENTURE CAPITAL*

We are still building the foundation of our knowledge in venture capital. Since we're now aware of our local entrepreneurial ecosystem, we need to develop an opinion on the overall venture capital landscape. What is the best way to quickly develop a perspective that takes years of experience?

Use the wisdom of others that came before you.

## Blogs

That's right. Venture capital blogs offer an incredible opportunity for you to gain insight in the investor process. The goal here—which we'll discuss in-depth later in the book—is to answer the interview question, "Can you tell me something that's going on in the industry?" Some of my favorite blogs are:

## Paul Graham

Paul Graham is someone who tends to make bold statements about innovation and the economics of technology. He co-founded Y-Combinator and what would later become Yahoo! Store. As someone who studied painting and computer science, he writes from a unique perspective as is displayed in *Hackers & Painters* and his well-known essays.

"How to Start a Startup" offered me a basic toolkit to grasp that people, great execution and understanding what the customer really wants, are more important than a brilliant idea. "Why Smart People Have Bad Ideas" let me know that although some founders can seem promising, they may have simply chosen the wrong problem to solve and it may be best to wait for their next new iteration—or business—entirely.

"Do Things That Don't Scale" taught me the importance of the 'dirty work' startups have to accomplish in the early days, like focusing on a deliberately narrow market to test the product or going out of their way to acquire users, and make them happy with insane attention-to-detail as if they're a consultant with only one client.

These are just three of the 174 essays currently on Paul's site. There are a few resources that summarize the content or present a "Top 10," but at this stage I think the best move is to read the above blogs and a few other articles where the title catches your eye.

### Mark Suster

Mark Suster is a prominent blogger-turned-VC who was able to sell two businesses along the way. He often gives really clear, yet eye-opening insights into tech and venture investing. Mark wrote one of my all-time favorite articles, "Invest in Lines, Not Dots" where he very simply states that every time you connect with a VC, mentor or advisor, your company should have achieved some sort of perceived progress and be farther along than the last encounter. Novel advice, but this forms the basis of your relationship with a VC, or anyone for that matter.

VCs are often investing in people over companies. Even if a VC doesn't invest in an entrepreneur whose business eventually fails, if they showed progress with every pitch meeting, an investor still knows their capabilities and would likely be happy to work with them on their next business.

### Jason Calacanis

Jason Calacanis is a prolific blogger, entrepreneur and angel investor who sold two businesses and currently operates the LAUNCH Conference and newsletter, the Inside network of newsletters and the *This Week in Startups* show. Aside from the wealth of information LAUNCH, Inside and *This Week in Startups* provide, Jason continues to personally blog on his site.

Articles like "What I learned from passing on investing in Twitter & Zynga — & saying yes to Uber & Thumbtack" reinstate Paul Graham's thoughts on just how important people, particularly founders, are to the success of a company.

In "Snapchat is going to reach a billion users thanks to 'Gen-S' — the smartphone generation", Jason asserts precisely how Snapchat is going to challenge larger platforms through a DJ Khaled case study, ascribing the low cost of content production and high viewership (at the date of his post, DJ Khaled snaps amassed just as many views as an episode of *Keeping Up with the Kardashians*) to the platform's inevitable long-term success.

### Fabrice Grinda

Fabrice Grinda is a French entrepreneur and investor with over $300M in exits and 200 investments. He often blogs about venture investing and emerging tech trends. His "Macro perspective: The startup party is far from over!" article made me realize that venture-backed startups are staying private twice as long as they did in the 1990s because the cost to stay private these days has greatly decreased as capital becomes more accessible. He goes on to say that compliance burdens limit liquidity for small companies, and have also increased the cost of going public.

### Sam Altman

Sam Altman is the current president of Y-Combinator and was previously a founder at Loopt, which sold to Green Dot Corporation for $43M. As head of YC, Sam often dispenses an entire guide's worth of information through his blog. Sam's "Startup Playbook" will walk you through everything a great startup should have from ideation to product instantiation, and is an invaluable tool for aspiring venture investors.

Additionally, Sam's been kind enough to host the 20-episode video series, *How to Start a Startup*—originally a lecture at Stanford—on his blog. The series includes talks from luminaries like Paul Graham, Marc Andreessen of Andreessen Horowitz and Reid Hoffman, founder of LinkedIn.

### Kanyi Maqubela

Kanyi Maqubela was a founding employee at Doostang, and is now a partner at Collaborative Fund, an early stage firm that often prioritizes culture, creativity and value when seeking investment opportunities. In "Entrepreneurs Need a Better Way to Cash Out", I learned about venture debt, or debt capital, as a way to scale startups with cash flow and allow them to grow until equity financing is absolutely necessary.

His "Why the Collaborative Economy is an Impact Economy" post and his speech at the Clinton Global Initiative touch upon the ways in which we can leverage our current economy—the collaborative or "shared economy" where global decentralized communication is the new norm—through mission-driven companies without compromising profit.

## CB Insights

Anand Sanwal and the folks at *CB Insights* (a great subscription idea for students), aside from being an amazing resource in itself to learn about leading and emerging companies in a sector, have put together a wonderful list of VC blogs.

I stumbled on a few of the blogs above after glancing at *CB Insights'* "Periodic Table of Venture Capital Blogs." Try to read maybe two or three articles per blogger until you start to feel you can develop a perspective on the industry and where it's headed.

## Podcasts

Another great resource is podcasts, but these generally take time to sift through. I think the best all-around podcast comes from the heavyweights at Andreessen Horowitz (stylized as "a16z").

The a16z podcast has become a true force in understanding any given sector through interviews with thought leaders and great entrepreneurs in their space. I began to develop an interest in the bitcoin blockchain protocol, how it works, and if a blockchain network independent of bitcoin (or any other currency) could really exist in the long-term.

Aside from the incredible reporting and research coming out of the CoinDesk news site, there seems to be no better resource than a16z's interview with the CEO of Chain, Adam Ludwin. In a16z's "Blockchain vs./and Bitcoin," Adam explained what bitcoin is, its limitations, and how blockchain can prosper and create decentralized networks for other financial instruments and stores of value like merchant-issued currency (gift card transfer), airtime on a mobile phone, energy credits on a grid and even tokens for machine-to-machine communication as we enter into the internet-of-things (IoT) and the autonomous vehicle era.

The Product Hunt, Rocketship.fm and Accidental Creative podcasts are also not bad places to start.

## Deals

A favorite question for VCs is "Can you tell me about an interesting deal in the past year?" The CrunchBase Daily e-mail, Fortune Magazine's Term Sheet and the *StrictlyVC* blog are great sources for information on daily deals. You may come across large deals that industry folks are discussing (2015: Snapchat's $500M Series E, Uber's $1.2B round funded by Baidu, Zenefits' $500M Series C). Keep an eye on deals like these and start to search for opinion pieces on each.

For instance, are investors concerned about Snapchat's long-term profitability? How exactly will Baidu's investment in Uber help growth in China? Are investors concerned about Zenefits' low revenue now that it reached *unicorn* ($1B+ valuation) status?

Through reading Term Sheet in early 2016, I realized the impact of mutual funds on tech valuations. If public mutual funds like Fidelity or T. Rowe Price mark down the value of their private technology shares in companies like Dropbox or Zenefits, it could signal a weak IPO market and unreliably high valuations that the public markets will not be able to absorb.

Reading daily news will offer up informed opinions on the tech sector that will enhance your knowledge of the venture space, and inevitably make you stand out when encountering VCs.

## Events

Events are a shortcut to connecting and networking with venture capitalists, as well as entrepreneurs, and help you to land a job in the industry. Since VCs go to events and pitch festivals to find new companies, so should you. There are always startup events to attend.

Startups will often attend or sponsor tech events and a few may have interesting products or founders. If you find a company intriguing, the odds are good that a venture capitalist will as well. Always reach out to the entrepreneur to get their contact information and have a few questions ready about their startup.

Networking with entrepreneurs is a useful skill in becoming a VC. If you land an interview with a seed stage venture capital firm or an *accelerator*, who works with a company at the earliest stages of their lifecycle, you'll have a great opportunity to showcase your knowledge of the space, and answer the "What's your favorite startup?" question.

# Chapter 5
# GROWTH EQUITY
*WHAT IT IS AND EVERYTHING YOU NEED TO KNOW ABOUT BREAKING IN*

## What is Growth Equity?

*Growth equity* refers to investing in a company at later rounds (Series C, D, E, etc.) in order to have the company either IPO or get acquired. Strategic buyers (actual companies like General Motors, Google and Microsoft) do most major acquisitions, but it's also common to see a private equity firm (Blackstone, The Apollo Group, KKR etc.) acquire an entire company as well. Growth equity investments can range from $10M to $500M or higher as some growth equity firms experiment with majority buyouts.[2]

The target companies here have at least $5M in revenue, 20 percent revenue growth in the last few years or higher, a proven business model and a clear pathway to becoming a profitable company.[3] Now that we've covered the lifecycle of a startup we can begin to visualize what the funding spectrum looks like.

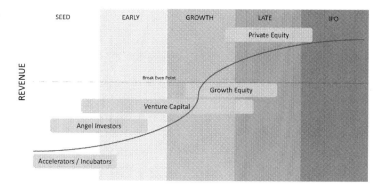

To recap, angels and accelerators are usually the first money in and deploy capital in exchange for equity after the company has a working prototype or viable product. The most prominent accelerators in the US are Y-Combinator and Techstars.

Some of the most noted angel investors are Alexis Ohanian (founder of Reddit), Marc Benioff (founder of Salesforce) and Max Levchin (founder of Paypal, Slide and Affirm) who on occasion invest in early stage and growth rounds as well. If the core product of the business begins to gain market share, and it seems the company has a lasting opportunity to scale and become an emerging leader, investors like First Round Capital and 500 Startups step in at the seed or Series A round.

Growth equity firms like Stripes Group, General Atlantic and Insight Venture Partners typically come in at the Series C or D stage when the business becomes the number one or two player in the industry and is ripe for an IPO or strategic acquisition.

In the event that the business needs additional capital either for global expansion or future acquisitions, some of the larger institutional or private equity players like Tiger Global Management or Fidelity may lead additional rounds beyond a Series D. These rounds are typically more than $50M and can easily go into the billions.

**Breaking In**

In order to understand growth equity, it helps to have a foundation in accounting and basic valuation. Other than having a high-level understanding of financial analysis, it's crucial to understand the differences between venture capital, growth equity and private equity.

**Growth Equity and Venture Capital**

As we discussed earlier, growth equity refers to late-stage venture capital deals that will typically help the company reach the public markets (IPO) or get acquired by a strategic company or financial sponsor. Additionally, there are some core differences between venture capital and growth equity that you will need to understand before reaching out to firms.

## Investment Thesis

A venture capital firm invests under the premise of an *upside scenario*, this is to say that if the firm invests in 10 companies through the fund, they only expect one or two companies to hit a home run (an 8-10x return or more), and couple solid returns ( >1x), while the other six or seven companies may fail (no return) or simply return the amount invested (a 1x return). Of course, they'd like to see more successes but typically a venture capital firm only gains a return from a small portion of their investments.

Since these firms are investing at an earlier stage and have a high risk profile, early stage venture firms seek higher returns than growth equity firms. A target or anticipated cash-on-cash *return on investment (ROI)*, or multiple of the amount of cash invested, is typically 8-10x for early stage venture capital investors.[4, 5]

A quick seven-figure exit may suffice in venture capital, but it is simply not enough to generate positive returns in growth equity. In this space, late-stage investors will act only if they see the potential for a firm to become a market leader in their industry. In other words, while both venture capital and growth equity firms are looking for the next Seamless, Uber or Netflix, the evidence of a startup becoming a market leader needs to be much stronger in growth equity. Since the risk profile is relatively lower compared to traditional venture capital, target ROI here is a little lower and typically exists in the 3-5x range.[6]

## Target Company

Venture capital firms and angel groups would like to see the most developed product possible, but at this time in a company's history—the seed stage—typically the company has little-to-no customers, little revenue and may not have reached the *minimum viable product*, or MVP stage yet where they have a lean but substantial version of their product.

Growth equity firms will only target companies with a substantial revenue and customer base. Since growth equity firms are typically trying to find market leaders, certain metrics that we will dive into later will also become important.

## Growth Equity and Private Equity

At first glance these terms may seem similar, but just as there are clear differences between growth equity and venture capital, growth equity and private equity also have structurally different business models.

## Stake in the Company

The purpose of growth equity—and venture capital for that matter—is to help companies hit certain milestones while leaving *equity*, or an owner's claim on the business, left over for future financing rounds (Series A, B, C etc.). Therefore, these firms must take a *minority stake*, or less than 50 percent in the company. In growth equity, these deals often range from $10M to $500M.

Private equity relies on a wholly different business model. Private equity firms like Blackstone, The Apollo Group and KKR will typically take a 100 percent stake, or complete ownership in an operational company. These firms will then scale that company through add-on acquisitions and organic growth for a period of 4 to 7 years until ultimately selling the company off to a strategic buyer.

These deals are typically anywhere from a few million to tens of billions with one of the largest strategy tech acquisitions of 2015 being NXP Semiconductor's $16.7B acquisition of Freescale Semiconductors, a company previously owned by The Blackstone Group, Carlyle and TPG Capital.[7]

## Cash Flow of the Target Company

Although growth equity firms invest only in companies that have a certain revenue profile, often times the business is not yet profitable or on the brink of becoming profitable. As a result, the business does not have a lot of pocket change, or spending money. Another way to say this is that growth equity companies tend to have lower *free cash flow (FCF)*, or money that is left over after "core expenses" like paying employees, advertising and keeping the lights on.

Private equity firms typically take out very sizable loans to buy a company. The loan represents the majority of the acquisition price while cash represents the other 30 to 40 percent of the investment. This model is referred to as a *leveraged buyout (LBO)* and as a result of this tactic, firms actually rely on companies that have a lot of pocket change, or high free cash flow.[8]

The process works like this: private equity firms look for companies with a high free cash flow, great management and strong consistency in sales. When a firm becomes interested, they execute an LBO in order to purchase a company and then transfer that *debt*, or money owed, to the target company. They will then use the free cash flow of the company they just bought in order to pay down the debt.

## Financing

Working off our understanding of cash flow, we can now see that private equity firms and growth equity firms not only have different business models but also different investment styles.

Growth equity firms will typically write a check in order to gain a stake in the company. This is typically called e*quity financing*, or writing a check for equity.

Since deal sizes are so large in private equity, firms really can't afford to write billion dollar checks every few months, so they use *debt financing*, the act of taking out a loan in order to purchase a company.

Of course, there are many more minute differences between these three asset classes, but if you are asked to differentiate between them, understanding the major differences in the above topics will serve you well.

# Chapter 6
# VENTURE DEBT
*WHAT IS IT AND HOW DOES IT WORK?*

I lied a little bit. Private equity firms aren't the only firms that use debt financing. In some instances, growth firms may actually prefer lending money to a company instead of writing a check for equity.

## History of Venture Debt

Venture capital as an industry is not that old, so the notion of venture-based debt financing, or *venture debt* is a fairly new concept. In the 1980s, if a technology company needed to build a factory or buy several pieces of equipment, companies preferred to take out loans instead of giving equity away for something that was not directly linked to hitting the next milestone.[9]

As the growth equity industry developed over time, venture debt became a standard way to push a company forward and an alternative to equity financing in many instances.

## When Does Venture Debt Happen?

Let's present a simple scenario. You are a founder at a tree-selling startup. Customers order their preferred tree through your app and your company delivers it to their house. As you're reaching profitability, Amazon decides to partner with you for the holiday season and now that we have access to more customers, the demand for trees skyrockets. Sounds great, what's the problem?

The problem is that you likely do not have the infrastructure or resources to supply that many trees to your customers. In other words, you can't meet the demand for trees. So, what do you do now?

Well, do you really want to raise money and have less of a stake in your company simply because your company is doing well? No, you would prefer to wait until capital is needed in order to hit a significant milestone like expanding in the Southwest, or going international.

As a result, you'll go to your growth investors and ask for a short-term loan. This is a typical scenario for venture debt. Now you'll be able to hire enough people to meet demand for the holiday season and then pay it back early next year without letting go of your share in the company. The equity you would have lost in equity financing can now be deployed to hit significant milestones in the future.

## Caveats

Some companies and even growth equity firms tend to have reservations when it comes to venture debt financing. As a prospective growth equity investor, it is unattractive for a company to have any debt at all. The longer a company is saddled with debt, the more difficult it becomes to raise money for the next round of financing.

Contracts for debt financing can also contain *debt covenants*, or requirements that a company may need to follow every quarter or risk defaulting on the loan. Such covenants usually require a company to hit certain performance metrics.

Now if another recession, downturn or any other macroeconomic factors occur that affect your business, you may not be able to keep up with those performance metrics the firm set in place. In addition to the risk of default, this may have a worrying social ripple effect for your current investors and prospective investors in your space.

Debt covenants may also offer *downside protection*, or the mitigation of loss in the event of *material adverse changes*, or significant events. Essentially, this means if you lose your main customer, the lead investor backs out of a deal, or any other number of crises occur, a firm may not be obligated to move further with the debt financing or the debt already issued may become immediately due.

For the firm, venture debt is only an option if the business is cash flow positive and shows strong signs of revenue consistency. Growth firms also tend to not provide debt financing to firms that already have debt on their balance sheet. Typically, firms only provide venture debt for companies that have balance sheet debt under 20 percent of operating expenses.

Since future incomes must be used in order to pay down the debt, seeing venture debt on a balance sheet can be considered risky to prospective investors.[10]

## Benefits

Although venture debt does have its drawbacks, securing cash through debt is sometimes in the best interest of both the entrepreneur and the investor.

The thesis of a growth firm is to give capital to a company so they can hit milestones and continually unlock value. That value is realized in future rounds of financing or through the sale of that company at a premium.

If we really break down venture debt, it allows a company to accelerate towards the next milestone with the application of quick cash, and increases the likelihood of actually reaching that milestone, all while minimizing the equity dilution that would inevitably occur with another round of equity financing.

Entrepreneurs can further understand the value of venture debt through their retained ownership of equity that otherwise would have been lost with another venture round.

As in our tree startup example, venture debt is a fairly common tool that allows a company to meet sales demand without giving away equity. Companies may also consider venture debt after they have raised a round and need a little more cash to accelerate growth.

Analysts estimate that the yearly volume of venture debt is between $2B to $4B, but these numbers are rough since most of the data is private.[11]

Venture debt often has entitlements, or *warrants*, for stock that allows the debt to convert into equity within the given timeframe. Depending on the terms, this can be seen as a more viable option for firms and companies.

Let's also look at the two main methods of investing here: debt and equity financing. As a company, what is the cost of doing debt financing? Well the cost of debt financing is the interest you will pay on the debt; let's say it's 10 to 15 percent. Now what is the cost of equity? Well, it's limitless since equity is considered a claim on future earnings and founders are always confident their company is going to skyrocket, right?

From an entrepreneurial perspective, debt financing is cheaper than equity financing because the cost of obtaining cash through debt is relatively less expensive. With debt financing an entrepreneur can increase *runway*—or the amount of venture money they've raised—and accelerate growth without worrying about losing any stake in their company.[12]

## The Right Mix

If a company's cash flow is unpredictable or they have not yet established a solid brand, equity financing can serve the purpose of reaching that particular milestone allowing the business to focus directly on growth and expansion. If a company needs to buy new equipment tied to revenue like a data center, new inventory, or seasonal labor to meet demand, then debt financing may work from an investor perspective.

Finding the right mix of venture debt and equity financing can often lead to incredible growth opportunities for a company. After establishing several brand partnerships, a company may be unwilling to dilute more equity, and venture debt could be the only option. If revenue is very high and lots of money is coming in, then a simple *line of credit* might be a better option than venture debt.[13]

# Chapter 7
# PERFORMANCE METRICS
*BLENDING IN DURING THE INTERVIEW*

Like any other industry, venture capital has its own language and terminology. The interviewer isn't only looking to see if you can answer their questions, they are also looking to see if you can pitch startups to vice presidents, principals and partners as if you've been following the industry for years.

The best way to go about blending into the industry through an interview is to make use of key industry terms and use them in the correct context. I outline some terms here to start off. These should get you through the interview, but I urge you to look up additional terms as you begin to analyze companies.

### Monthly Recurring Revenue (MRR)

When a company accounts for all the revenue in a given month that is contractually obligated to recur next month, that is *monthly recurring revenue (MRR)*. So, if a *Software-as-a-Service (SaaS)* business, otherwise known as a business that licenses their software to others on a subscription basis, has 40 annual subscriptions with clients valued at $12,000 per contract, we can normalize the annual contract on a monthly recurring basis to arrive at a monthly recurring revenue stream of $40,000. $1,000 for the normalized monthly charge on the contract multiplied by the 40 customers.

### Annualized Run Rate (ARR)

Investors often want the most accurate depiction of a company's yearly revenue. The optimal method in early stage businesses is to take the monthly recurring revenue (MRR) of a business and multiply it by 12 to arrive at the *annualized run rate (ARR)*.

Annualized Run Rate (ARR) = Monthly Recurring Revenue (MRR)  * 12

In the above example the ARR is the MRR ($40,000) multiplied by 12, or $480,000.[14]

## Churn Rate

*Churn rate* usually refers to the attrition rate of customers—or number of customers lost—in a given period, but it can be used in other instances as well (employees, board members, dollars retained and other scenarios). If a company's annual churn rate increased from 5 percent to 8 percent, they've lost 8 percent of their customers in the period. The term *logo churn* is also synonymous with churn rate in this sense. All else equal, it's better have a lower customer churn rate.

If you tend to see the word "churn" after any term it likely reflects a percentage loss in that particular category.

## Calculating Customer Churn Rate

Since we are calculating a churn *rate*, we need two periods: the old period (last year) and the new period (this year). From here, we'll take all the customers we lost in that timeframe and divide by the number of customers we had at the beginning of the year.

That means if our tree selling startup, *TreeCo* had 1000 customers at the beginning of the year and 800 customers at the end, TreeCo lost 200 customers throughout the year, a 20 percent annual churn.

(1000 – 800) / 1000 = 200 / 1000 = 20 percent annual customer churn

Is this a big churn or a small churn? Well, that depends on the industry, but losing 20 percent of your customers is a big deal for any company! A study by Bessemer Venture Partners notes that an acceptable annual customer churn rate is anything below 7 percent, which comes out to about a .58 percent monthly churn.[15]

## Using the Term

Here's a quick example of how to incorporate churn rate into your company analysis.

> *I know TreeCo is thinking of expanding into second-tier cities like Miami and Raleigh, but I'd love to inquire to management about their current churn in San Francisco and New*

*York. There's a lot of local and brand name competition in these cities and I'm curious about the strategies they're employing to stop the potential loss of customers and ultimately, revenue.*

## Burn Rate

*Burn rate* refers to the amount of venture capital cash used or "burned" in a given period by a startup. Think of burn rate as the churn rate of a startup's money that came from funding. You'll often hear this term conversationally—as in a high or low burn rate—but the calculation is quite similar to churn rate; we'll just divide the difference by the number of periods (usually months).

The whole idea here is to figure out how fast a business is burning through money so the company can determine the most optimal time to raise a new round. The burn rate also gives the investor a more thorough understanding of how a company is managing money.

## Calculating Burn Rate

Take the total venture cash you have at the beginning of the period and the amount you have at the end. Divide that difference by the number of actionable months.

Let's imagine TreeCo just received a $250,000 investment in January of this year. But after about 8 months they only have $75,000 dollars left. What's their burn rate?

($250,000 - $75,000) / 8 months = $175,000 / 8 months = $21,875 per month

Now TreeCo knows that at this current rate they are spending about $22,000 per month with only $75,000 left. At this rate, they'll be out of money before the end of the year and will need more *runway*, or venture capital money to stay afloat.[16]

## Using the Term

Since the burn rate of a company is not typically public knowledge, you'll often hear this term applied to an array of startups in a particular industry or sector.

*Companies in the crowdsourced food and transportation space compete heavily to acquire customers. As a result of such high sales and marketing spend, the typical burn rate of*

*companies in these industries is notoriously high. So much so, that in the past it has made sense for companies in the same industry—like Seamless and Grubhub or Didi and Kuadi, the two taxi hailing apps in China—to merge.*

## Dollar Revenue Retention (DRR)

*Dollar revenue retention* refers to the amount of revenue you are retaining from your customers in a given period. The metric is largely used in the Software-as-a-Service (SaaS) industry and others that have tiered pricing.

DRR serves as a more precise way to measure success from a revenue perspective as opposed to churn rate.

## Explaining the Term

Since dollar revenue retention is a fairly new term, let's talk about it in context before we do any calculations.

Imagine a company that writes software to retrieve and store data from a computer system, otherwise known as a database management system. This software company sells its services to other companies using a tiered pricing strategy.

There is an entry-level price where the customer has access to the most popular features, a premium tier which gives the customer access to almost all of the software's features, and an advanced tier where customers can adapt the software exactly to their needs.

Let's say that some customers are paying $50 for the premium set of features while others are paying $25 for the entry-level set of features.

Pop quiz: if we have two customers and they're both on the premium plan, but all of a sudden one moves to the entry-level plan. What is the churn rate?

The churn rate is 0 percent because no customers have left the business. The one customer just downgraded to a cheaper plan and as a result the software company retains less revenue. Dollar revenue retention exists to measure and better understand these situations.[17]

## Calculating Dollar Revenue Retention

Let's consider a cohort example with two customers, Hank and Todd. Hank loves the premium software plan and pays $50 per month for the majority of the database management system's features. Meanwhile, Todd feels that his small business only needs the basics and pays the bare minimum entry-level price at $25.

> Year One
> Hank: $50 (Premium)
> Todd: $25 (Entry-level)
> Total: $75

In the second year, Hank's company grows and he makes the decision to sign on for the advanced tier at $100 while Todd's company got acquired and the parent company now does database management in-house.

> Year Two
> Hank: $100 (Advanced)
> Todd: Cancelled
> Total: $100

If we take the new revenue from this cohort in year two, $100 and divide it by the old revenue from year one, we'll have a figure for the dollars retained from period one to period two, or dollar revenue retention.

$$\$100y2 / \$75y1 = 133 \text{ Dollar Revenue Retention}$$

Think for a second about the churn rate here, what does it tell us about the business? Well, the churn rate is 50 percent so if we're analyzing the company using this metric alone we're not getting much information, but DRR tells the real story that we've actually upgraded Hank to advanced.

## Thoughts on Dollar Revenue Retention and Customer Churn Rate

If you could only optimize one of these metrics, which would you choose?

Say the industry average annual customer churn is 6 percent and your SaaS company is at 8 percent, but your dollar revenue retention is 110 percent. Can this be a good thing?

Absolutely yes. Like our example above, what likely happened is the company started to focus and market their software towards the small percentage of customers that are paying more for the advanced plan. Over this period, some of the entry-level customers left while advanced customers signed on.

It's always important to look beneath the surface. A small increase in churn is not necessarily a bad thing, if the dollar revenue retention increases as a result.

If the reverse happens—a drop in DRR below 100 percent and a lower churn—current customers are likely downgrading and finding more value in the entry-level product.

Together, dollar revenue retention and churn rate help establish the bigger picture for a company.[18]

## Dollar Revenue Retention and Revenue Churn Rate

Since churn measures a loss over time, dollar revenue retention rate can also be measured through *revenue churn*, or the measure of lost revenue over time.

The formula will be identical to customer churn, except we will use revenue in a given year instead of the number of customers.

$$(\$75y1 - 100y2) / \$75y1 = -33 \text{ percent annual revenue churn}$$

Here, a revenue churn of −33 percent means the company gained revenue year one to year two.

## Customer Lifetime Value (CLV)

*Customer lifetime value* (CLV) represents the projected revenue that a customer will bring for a company during their lifetime as a customer. Since customer acquisition and marketing can be expensive, metrics like CLV help determine just how much a company can spend to acquire a customer beforehand. If a company is spending more than CLV to acquire a customer, they may actually lose money in the long run.

Now all customers aren't created equal and there are a few ways to measure CLV so we'll work with the easiest method since you really only need to be familiar with the term.

## Calculating Customer Lifetime Value

The simplest way to calculate customer lifetime value is to work with the variable averages. That way no matter how many customers we have we'll simply use the average to represent each variable. To calculate CLV we'll start with average customer revenue per visit (e), average number of visits per week (n) and average customer value per week (e * n).

Using a delivery service app that takes a fee per delivery order as an example, let's say the average revenue from a customer after delivery is $4 per visit (e) and the average customer visits the site 3 times a week (n). We can now calculate the average customer value per week as $20 (e*n).

Average Customer Revenue per Visit (e): $4

Average Number of Visits per Week (n): 3

Average Customer Value per week (e*n): $12

Now that we have the customer value per week, how do we find the customer value for a lifetime? Well let's measure the lifespan in years so we can start by multiplying average customer value per week by 52.

Average customer lifespan, or how long someone intends to be a customer is crucial to CLV calculation. We can likely grab this figure from an analyst report on a similar company in the industry, but let's say that average customer lifespan is 25 years.

Lastly, since we only talked about revenue so far, we'll need to know the average profit margin per customer (p). The company can likely calculate this in-house or grab a comparable from a similar company. Let's say average profit margin per customer is 20 percent. Now we're ready to find customer lifetime value.

> Customer Lifetime Value (Simple Calculation)
> 52 * Average Customer Value per Week * Average Customer Lifespan
> 52 * e * n * 25 * p = 52 * 12 * 25 * .20 = $3,120 Customer Lifetime Value

The delivery app company now knows the exact value of a single customer over their lifetime. If marketing and acquisition costs exceed $3,120 per new customer, the company will lose money in the long run despite onboarding more customers in the short run.

There are many other ways to understand and measure CLV and because of this you likely won't be asked to calculate CLV in an interview, but the term is used considerably when doing due diligence on early stage companies.[19]

## Using the Term

I use CLV in the Udemy case study, but will lay out a simple scenario below.

> In health care, an overall positive outcome is determined by patient effort and doctor effort. If digital health companies find ways to further engage patients and increase the number of positive outcomes, they can count on an increased number of visits in a given period and an overall higher customer lifetime value.

Feel free to use customer lifetime value in relation to customers buying into a service more frequently (increasing "n", or average number of visits per week) or decreasing any costs directly related to acquiring or maintaining customers (decreasing costs increases "p", or average profit margin per customer).

## Customer Acquisition Cost (CAC)

We implicitly touched on *customer acquisition cost (CAC)* when discussing CLV, it is simply the cost of acquiring a new customer. Costs typically tucked into CAC are advertising, PR, base pay for sales people as well as commission, sales manager salaries, any on-boarding costs and any other business or industry-specific costs. The lower your CAC, the better.[20]

## Calculating Customer Acquisition Costs

To simplify this calculation, we can let CAC equal the sales and marketing costs in the income statement divided by the number of new customers acquired in a given period. Using our delivery service app example, let's say the sales and marketing budget is $300,000 and this allows us to get 300 new customers. This yields a CAC of $1000.

$300,000 / 300 new customers = $1,000 CAC

It's always beneficial to ask for a startup's customer acquisition cost, the lower the CAC the better. Now that we have a set number for customer lifetime value (CLV) and customer acquisition costs (CAC), we can combine the two into one metric to learn a little more about the company.

## Customer Lifetime Value to Customer Acquisition Cost Ratio (CLV/CAC Ratio)

Let's distill the *CLV/CAC ratio* into its key components.[21] The ratio is telling us that for every dollar the company spends on acquiring a new customer, the company will generate 'x' in value over the lifetime of that customer. Since this ratio reveals value, the higher the CLV/CAC ratio, the better off the company. All else being equal, an ideal company has a low customer acquisition cost and a high customer lifetime value. Let's calculate the CLV/CAC ratio for our delivery service app.

CLV/CAC Ratio
CLV/CAC = $3,120 / $1,000 = 3.13

We arrive at a CLV/CAC ratio of 3.12, or 3.12:1, but how can we benchmark this number and understand if the company is performing well or poorly? VCs love to see a CLV/CAC ratio nearing 3:1, essentially saying that company gets 3 dollars of value for every dollar it takes to acquire a new customer. Definitely a winning formula!

If the ratio is too small (1.5:1 or 1:1), the company is probably spending too much on acquiring customers and really needs to analyze their sales and marketing strategy. Anything over 3:1 can either be seen as a positive only in the short-term, or a sign that the company may be spending too little and missing out on business, a potential sign they may want to ramp up sales and marketing spend in the near future.

The more you understand what drives a great business, the more value you can add as an investor to help that business grow. If a company can't get their CLV/CAC ratio close to 3:1, or even worse if it's less than 1:1, it may be time to throw in the towel or pivot to another business model. CLV/CAC is somewhat of a sector-agnostic *key performance indicator (KPI)*, or business metric to help understand the effectiveness of a company. While it usually applies to software companies, it can also just as easily apply to companies in the Internet and Branded Consumer Products space.[22]

## CAC Payback Period

The *CAC payback period* is simply how long it takes to recover the cost of acquiring a customer. Ideally, we are looking for startups that can recoup this cost in 12 months or less. If there's a startup where the average customer brings in $10,000 over a lifetime of 50 months—or $200 per month—we'll want that company to not pay more than $2,400 ($200 * 12) to acquire that customer. If the company can accomplish a CAC payback period inside of 12 months, everything beyond that $2,400 can be reinvested back into the company.[23]

As investors, a 12-month payback period in the above example tells us that we can give this company $2,400 right now to acquire a customer and they can return an additional $7,600 dollars in 50 months.

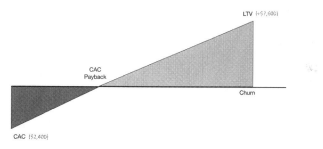

The faster the payback period, the more profit a company can gain in the long term. You can also view shorter payback periods as a manner in which entrepreneurs can retain equity in their company. More profits can now be invested back into the company and will push back the need for capital as well as any ownership dilution in the business.[24]

## Takeaways

We now understand some of the terms venture capitalists use and how to incorporate them into common startup scenarios. Terms like monthly recurring revenue (MRR) may seem opaque at first but it's just the sum of all the contract revenue on the table that a business can rely on for the next month. Take that amount and multiply by 12 to get the annualized run rate (ARR), or what a business may likely take in during the course of a year.

If a business loses customers, we can now turn that into a metric (churn rate) and benchmark it against an industry average. If the churn rate goes up slightly but most customers upgrade to a higher pricing tier, we can use dollar revenue retention to better understand business performance on a YoY (year-over-year) basis.

If we're thinking of investing in a company, the burn rate will tell us how much cash a business typically spends in a given month or year while the customer life time value to customer acquisition cost ratio (CLV to CAC ratio) will tell us how many dollars are brought in (cash inflow) for every dollar spent on sales and marketing to acquire a customer (cash outflow). These terms provide a strong foundation for understanding business performance in early to late stage startup businesses.

# Chapter 8
# AN INDUSTRY THAT EXCITES YOU
## *HOW TO UNDERSTAND ANY MARKET*

A popular question that VCs often ask is "Can you tell me about an industry that excites you?" They will then lead the conversation into a pitch about a particular company in the industry.

The important thing here is to understand they are not only searching for your intuitive understanding of the question, but also a high-level analysis of the concerns and benefits, or *headwinds* and *tailwinds* of the company.

### The Space

When discussing your chosen industry, make sure you know a few things that will impart your knowledge of the space like market size, recent funding, firms with the most investment and any positive trends or tailwinds, like the regulatory landscape in a region the company wishes to expand.

### How to Understand Any Market

Understanding the *TAM (Total Addressable Market)* and what the industry as a whole is projected to look like in a few years, can go a long way. There are a few ways to do this. I'll list the methods that have worked best for me in the past.

### Library Resources

If you are a student at an accredited university, you will have access to your university's library, which in turn will have a subscription to business publications and peer-reviewed journals. If the company is well-documented, any material events occurring in the past two years will be easily accessible. Spend a few hours taking notes on these events and be ready to express them in the interview.

Do a database or Google search for your industry's market size or search for a specific startup in the market. You should be able to find this information fairly easily.

When searching for market size you will often find reports by research firms with price tags of over $1,000, please do not pay for these. Instead, run a simple ctrl+f search for "market size" or go over to the summary tab, you should find ample information here.

## Useful Websites

Sites like *CB Insights*, *Markets and Markets*, *SIIA* and *Statista* can help you arrive at ballpark estimates of a given market and solid estimates of projected growth.

Try to have two references here to reinforce the market information you use in interviews. If the above sites do not work for you, google "edtech market size" or whatever market you are researching and you will likely find several reports or small pdfs that will have this information.

If the company in question is at the Series A stage or below, you can always use Google News to find recent articles about the company that may lead to an analyst's assessment of market size.

## Funding

Let's take edtech (education technology) for example, has there been an increase in funding in the edtech space in the past five years? Yes, according to a quick Google search and *CB Insights*, apparently, there has been a 500 percent increase in edtech funding from 2010 to 2015.

We can distill this information even further with exact figures if they are available. Further research reveals that $900M was invested in edtech in 2013, whereas in 2015 $2B was invested in the edtech space.[25]

## Market Size

Additionally, *Markets and Markets* tells us that global education technology is about a $50B market and analysts estimate that it will continue to grow at about 17 percent annually from 2016 to 2020.[26]

## Additional Information

To layer your own insights on top of market data is always incredibly valuable. For instance, if a market does not have a current leader, this means there's room for a newer startup to take over. After doing 20 minutes of research through my school's database, I found out that there's no real Uber or Seamless of edtech and the market is considered highly fragmented.

This means there is room for consolidation or mergers among startups, and also presents an opportunity for any new entrants to become the market leader.

## Putting It All Together

Now we can synthesize all of our information into one simple paragraph to show off our knowledge.

> *There are a lot of interesting things going on in the edtech space. It's grown a lot in the past few years largely due to the increase in funding and I think the overall market will continue grow. Also, I think there's a real opportunity here because there is no real industry leader that is miles ahead.*

I didn't use exact figures here because an interview is similar to a conversation. If I'm just talking to you about the edtech space I am not going to mention the figures we gathered from *CB Insights* and *Markets and Markets*; however, if you ask me about them I will definitely have the information ready.

The general rule about interviewing is to answer a question directly without dumping too much knowledge on the interviewer. If the interviewer asks, "What's an iPhone?" you can simply answer, "An iPhone is a device made by Apple" without going into all the applications and colors and technical information about the phone. The interviewer will dig deeper if they want to test your knowledge further, but clear and concise answers here are always best.

Chapter 9

# A COMPANY THAT EXCITES YOU

*HOW TO ANSWER THIS QUESTION*

Now that we know a little about edtech, let's discuss a company inside of the industry and find the best way to tackle this question.

After demonstrating your knowledge of edtech, the interviewer will probe further and ask you to discuss a company in the space. If you want to choose a company that the VC firm has funded, that is absolutely fine but not necessary unless you are prompted to do so.

## Udemy

Let's dive into an analysis of Udemy, one of the ten most well-funded companies in the edtech space as of the date of this publishing. I will write this as a script so you can gain a more in-depth understanding of how the pitch may sound.

## Udemy Market Size

*I see a lot of interesting things going on in the edtech space. It's grown a lot in the past few years largely because of the increase in funding and I believe the overall market will continue to grow. Almost a quarter of current college students take online courses on sites like Udemy and almost half of those students are putting those courses on their resume. It's an interesting time in the industry because I don't think there's any real industry leader here, like a Seamless or an Uber, that is miles ahead.*

Here, I've introduced the space and shared my thoughts on growth in a conversational manner. Again, I tend to feel a little less mechanical once I take out the actual numbers but you can always feel free to include them. As cited in the previous chapter, the "increase in funding" was 500 percent in the past five years and the global market size is $50B as of the date of this publication.

## How to Pitch a Company

In order to pitch a company, you need to be aware of their level of funding, key hires, material events and partners, what you admire about the company and your suggestions for management.

This information can be acquired in the same manner that we acquired information about the market size: *CB Insights*, your school library and Google News.

There is a certain structure that is nice to follow here. Introduce the company and a material event that has recently happened, like an expansion or perhaps a new partner. If you can, tie one of the new hires into that expansion. Discuss your ideas about how the company can leverage their expertise in "x" in order to affect some of the metrics mentioned earlier like achieving a higher customer lifetime value or a lower churn rate.

After you relate what is admirable about the company, include any high-level *headwinds* or caveats you may have for management and close with any of your personal thoughts about the company. I'll continue with the Udemy case study written as a script. It may appear a bit bulky but the idea is to craft a pitch like this and make it your own.

## Udemy Case Study

*Udemy raised $65M through their Series D round in 2015. I like the whole idea of blended learning, or digital and real life instruction, in a corporate setting. I know there's a huge market here and Udemy already has great clients like Oracle, Pepsi and Lyft. And now, with Darren Shimkus as the new head of Udemy for Business, I think Udemy is in a great place to really take over the space of training global knowledge workers.*

*I see their expansion on a global scale. I know half of their revenue comes from outside of the US and I don't think that's going to change. They signed on to work with some of the leading corporate training platforms in Singapore last year and in this regard, **it's fairly cheap to host and create a*** *curriculum, so I think as long as the economy is doing well and unemployment is low, **there's going to be a high customer lifetime value**, and they're arguably making the world a better and more efficient place, which is awesome.*

*Also, the great thing about global corporate training affiliates is **your churn rate is sort of institutionalized.** As long as you are putting a good product forward I think people will go from using Udemy at work to using these classes in their home, **another generator of high customer lifetime value.***

*But all that aside, with globalizing the corporate training model through blended learning, I would be curious to know Udemy's thoughts on the **digital literacy rate of prospective countries in the Middle East and regions in Africa** they'd like to move into. **I think that may be a potential headwind.***

*I'd also inquire about how macroeconomic factors can play into corporate training as well as **get their thoughts on maintaining a low churn rate over time**. Lastly, I know Udemy has 8 million students in over 200 countries, but **I'm curious to know how many business partnerships they have in those countries.***

*Overall, I think Udemy has an incredible opportunity to really take over the global corporate training market and it will be interesting to see how they maneuver and grow in the next few years.*[27, 28]

## Takeaways

You can see that the pitch is broken down into three parts: an introduction, tying in material events and hires to make careful assessments, and overall suggestions or questions for management.

I bolded my own insights in the pitch in order to show you what the VC on the other side of the interview is listening for. They likely know most of the details of what you are saying, but they're really trying to gauge your insights and conviction toward the company of your choosing as well as your genuine excitement for venture capital and their firm in particular.

The amount of original insight you can add is a great indicator of your passion in a given field. It will take you miles ahead of your competitors who are likely simplifying and recycling information from the above sources. Creating your own bolded insights above is one of the keys to being a cut above the rest in the interview process.

Chapter 10
# INTERVIEW QUESTIONS
*HOW TO ANSWER BASIC VC INTERVIEW QUESTIONS*

---

VCs will often ask fairly basic questions to make sure you have an understanding of the industry as a whole before asking you to pitch a company. We'll go over some of those questions here.

### Why X Firm?

Look at the team page and look at the managing partners. They will undoubtedly have a wealth of experience possibly going back to the dot-com era or even further. Regardless, speak on their experience and how this would be an incredible learning opportunity for you. Be sincere as well, if one of the partners had experience in fashion-tech and you see yourself working in that industry long term, don't be afraid to mention that.

If you have the opportunity to speak to entrepreneurs or other individuals who have knowledge of the firm, try to figure out some key differentiators. Perhaps they specialize in creating brand recognition for a startup or maybe they have unmatched expertise in recruiting or other expansion opportunities. If so, those aspects should be mentioned in response to the "Why X firm?" question as well.

### Why VC?

As we mentioned earlier there are key differences between venture capital (early stage investing) and growth equity (late stage investing). Although growth equity firms will sometimes refer to themselves as venture capitalists, this question explicitly refers to VCs as early stage investors.

It's best to give a short answer here:

I'd like to get my hands dirty and work and grow with a diverse set of companies from the ground up. I want to focus on strategy and early stage investing. I can't get that experience anywhere else and this is the best learning opportunity for me.

## Why Growth Equity? Why Not Private Equity?

Here, the interviewer is implicitly asking you "Why not VC" and "Why not private equity" so it's best to include these thoughts in your answer.

Growth equity is **built on finding market leaders like the next Seamless or Uber**, I think it would be an incredible opportunity to learn how to differentiate companies and understand what really makes a great company at scale.

When I think about the VC early stage model, **it's largely built around upside scenario**, where one or two companies can "make" the fund while the others are sort of expected to fail. To me, this model is **kind of like blindly throwing darts on a board expecting to hit the bullseye**, except the darts are really, really expensive. Although we expect some companies to fail in growth equity, it's nowhere near as many as in VC and for me personally, I feel this model provides the biggest learning opportunity to understand the industry at large.

I have some colleagues with experience in private equity and from what I understand, it seems to be about **making as much money as possible**, which doesn't sound like a bad thing, but **it's not always in the best interest of the company**. For example, a PE firm can execute a take-private and make this new portfolio company issue a dividend recap (recapitalization), which is essentially a dividend paid to the private equity firm and other shareholders. Dividend recaps are very popular in the space and it not only increases debt, **but it makes it really difficult to grow a new company**. It's also not unusual to hear of dividend recaps while portfolio companies are facing major layoffs.

*I believe more in the overall philosophy of growth equity investing and I can see myself working in this industry in the long term.*

## Takeaways

I bolded my own insights again so you can get a clear sense of what is really being asked. The interviewer wants to make sure you understand the difference between growth equity, VC and private equity while providing your own insights.

Talk about why you want to work in growth equity, talk about why not VC, hit some points on why not private equity as well and close with an emphasis on how much you would like to work in the growth equity space.

## Do You Have Any Questions for Me?

One of the most important questions they could possibly ask. This is your chance to really wow them by turning all of your knowledge in the industry into very pointed and particular questions.

## Typical Questions

Here are some typical questions that interviewees ask. These are your typical questions you will get from quick Google searches and odds are that your interviewers have heard them many times before.

*What's the difference between a good company and a great company?*

*Are there any big deals you guys missed out on? If so, what did you learn from them?*

These are ok questions and you'll receive a decent response from your interviewer. If you are talking to an analyst or associate, these questions may be fine. I'll talk about how to truly impress your interviewer below.

## Forward Your Questions for Management to the Interviewer

It is definitely your job to know some of the firm's portfolio companies fairly well. If you've reached the super day stage, you will speak with partners that are on the boards of portfolio companies as well as associates with expertise in that field.

If they happen to have expertise in the space you researched, *ask their thoughts on the future of the space*; even better, if they're on a board, relay your questions for the management team directly to the partner or associate. You can also simply ask what's next for the company with regard to a particular product or expansion. They'll really enjoy sharing what they can with you and it will create a memorable moment.

## Get Their Thoughts on the IPO Market

If they didn't ask you about the IPO markets in the interview, this is a great question to demonstrate your knowledge of the space. Below is an example:

> *Even though you had FitBit and Square IPOs which were nice, 2015 was one of the worst years for IPOS in the past 5 years. I think it had a little to do with Yellen and the Fed uncertainty there for a while and people having to hold off, or maybe the volatility in China. What are your thoughts on why 2015 was such a bad year for IPOs and what do you think we can expect in 2016? Is it going to be a more promising year?[29]*

## Get Their Thoughts on Longer IPO Time Horizons and Higher Valuations

The NVCA (National Venture Capital Association) recently reported that companies are going for IPOs later in their lifecycle (4-7 years) as opposed to previous years. Companies are also going for IPOs at much higher valuations than in past years. You can easily pose a question around these facts.

> *I'm noticing this trend and really just wanted to know your thoughts, if we go back to the 90s and look at few IPOS. Let's say Excite, around for about a year, IPOed at around $100M in the mid-90s. Amazon, around for about 3-4 years, IPOed for around $300M in the mid-90s. Then let's fast forward to 2015, we have companies like Box and Shopify that have been around for about ten years, IPOing in the low billions. Square's been around for 6 years, IPOed at like $3B. I was reading this NVCA report that companies are staying private for longer and waiting until higher valuations, like within the $1B to $3B range, to IPO.*

*My guess is that a lot of these guys got burned on both sides of the table in the dot-com bubble and wanted to sort of hold on to the fundamentals of the company, I'm wondering if this is more of a paradigm shift than a trend.*

*You guys have a ton of experience with scaling companies and IPOs, so I just wanted to know your thoughts on why is this happening?[30, 31, 32]*

I asked this question to a partner and he was quite surprised about my knowledge of IPOs in the past 20 years. He told me his thoughts on the matter, but the most important thing here was creating an opportunity to really differentiate myself from the competition.

### Get Their Thoughts on Being a Great Board Member

It's not often that you get to talk to someone who is on the board of a company. However in venture capital and growth equity you can easily find this information on their LinkedIn page. If they are a board observer, feel free to ask this question as well.

*I know you have the opportunity to sit on the boards of some amazing companies and that is definitely something I aspire to do. What makes a great board member? Is it simply doing no harm and staying out of the CEO's way or is there much more to it?*

### The Education of a VC

Venture capital and growth equity provide really unique opportunities to grow and learn what it's like to build a company, but it may take a really long time to learn the process. Feel free to ask what it is that VCs have actually learned.

*I know VC has one of the longest learning and feedback cycles since you don't often know if you've made a great investment until maybe 5 years or more out. I just wanted to ask, what's the education of a VC like? What have you learned in the past few years and who are you learning it from?[33]*

**Takeaways**

These are the types of question that create a memorable impression. Additionally, since these questions appear at the end of the conversation, your responses become a great way to save yourself if you feel like the interview is going a little south.

# Chapter 11
# FUNDAMENTALS OF ACCOUNTING
*A QUICK LESSON ON FINANCIAL STATEMENTS*

Don't panic. We're going to go over accounting at a very high level that will still allow you to impress venture capitalists in an interview setting. The three statements below are called financial statements and allow you to understand the inner workings, or financial activities of a company. For a more in-depth understanding of accounting I recommend two books: John Tracy's *How to Read a Financial Report* and Matan Feldman's *Crash Course in Accounting and Financial Statement Analysis*.

## Income Statement

The *income statement* is also referred to as the profit and loss (P&L) statement. The whole point of this statement is to understand the profitability of a company in a given period (usually a year or a quarter of a year).

## Gross Revenue

The top line of the income statement is known as sales, or gross revenue. This represents the money a company takes in from the sales of goods and services. If the company happens to be an e-commerce business like Seamless or a marketplace like Upwork, the top line of the income statement represents the total value of all transactions otherwise known as the *gross transaction value (GTV)*.

## Net Revenue

A marketplace can be defined as any 3rd party that connects supply (seller) and demand (buyer) while an e-commerce business—by definition—takes transactions online. In both types of businesses, the total flow of transactions, or the gross transaction value, does not go directly to the company. An e-commerce or marketplace business may only take 15 percent of GTV. That 15 percent is known as the *take rate* and becomes the *net revenue*, which goes directly to the company.

## Cost of Goods Sold (COGS)

*Cost of goods sold (COGS)*, or cost of sales are any expenses incurred for producing a good or service. This includes raw materials, labor or any manufacturing costs required to make all the products sold.

## Gross Profit and Gross Margin

Once you subtract COGS from net revenue, you end up with *gross profit*. Gross profit allows us to look at all the money we have left over to pay other expenses, which we'll talk about shortly.

The term *gross margin* is a profitability ratio. This metric is simply telling us the percentage of revenue that we will retain after the production of goods and services (COGS).

$$\text{Gross Margin (\%)} = \frac{\text{Revenue} - \text{Cost of Goods Sold}}{\text{Revenue}}$$

## Operating Expense (OPEX)

*Operating expenses* encompass several different cost buckets, namely sales, general and administrative expenses (SG&A) as well as research and development (R&D).

SG&A refers to the cost of advertising and marketing a product, keeping the lights on and executive salaries. Note that labor directly related to production would not fall into SG&A, as it's already accounted for in cost of goods sold.

R&D refers to general innovation practices. For instance, the iPhone 7 launched in 2016, but we can be certain that Apple is already at work developing the iPhone 8. The cost of employing these research scientists and engineers is R&D.

## Earnings Before Interest, Tax, Depreciation and Amortization (EBITDA)

Once we subtract OPEX from gross profit we arrive at another non-GAAP term known as *EBITDA*, or earnings before interest, tax, depreciation and amortization. As you can imagine many companies have different tax rates and ways to account for interest, thus making it difficult to compare one company with another. Think of this as comparing apples to oranges.

Since EBITDA represents earnings before all of these complications, we now have the ability to compare the earnings of companies in a more efficient manner. In other words, we can now compare apples with apples.

This term becomes more important and relevant in the chapter on valuation, but for now let's note its importance as a metric to evaluate a company. Most early stage and even growth stage technology companies will be EBITDA-negative, this is to say that COGS and OPEX will be greater than revenue. As a result, most technology companies are valued on multiples of revenue (e.g. 3x revenue), which I'll discuss in detail in the next chapter.

## Depreciation & Amortization (D&A)

Once we arrive at EBITDA we'll subtract what we refer to as *depreciation and amortization* (D&A). Since this is an expense outside of production (COGS and OPEX), it is referred to as a *non-operating expense*. Depreciation allocates the cost or decay of a physical asset over its lifetime. Amortization is the same principle applied to non-physical, or intangible assets like a patent. If you want to measure the cost of a truck over its lifetime you call this depreciation and if you want to measure the cost of a copyright on a particular product you call this amortization. The interviewer will likely use the term depreciation to apply to all of D&A.

There are many ways to measure D&A, but the most common is *straight-line depreciation*. With straight-line we simply take what we paid for the asset (cost of the asset) less what it would be worth at a scrap heap (salvage value) and then divide all of that by the useful life of the asset. This equation gives us the depreciation expense and we deduct this amount every period in our income statement for the life of the asset.

$$\text{Depreciation Expense} = \frac{\text{Cost of the Asset} - \text{Salvage Value}}{\text{Useful Life}}$$

## Operating Profit ≈ EBIT and Operating Margin

As you may have guessed, after subtracting D&A from EBITDA we end up with EBIT (earnings before interest and tax) which is commonly referred to as operating income or *operating profit* as well.

The accounting books that I referenced at the beginning of the chapter go into more depth here, but let's take a minute to note that operating profit is an SEC *generally accepted accounting principle (GAAP)* term, while EBIT is considered a non-GAAP term. There are minor differences between EBIT and operating income and you can read about them in the aforementioned books. I just wanted to take a second to establish this term and note that these two tend to be used interchangeably in the investing world.[34]

EBIT measures the earnings of a company before non-operating expenses like interest and taxes, which we'll talk about below.

Just as we have gross margin we also have *operating margin*. The operating margin represents the ratio of operating profit to revenue.

$$\text{Operating Margin} = \text{Operating Profit} / \text{Revenue}$$

### Interest Expense (or Income)

Companies will likely have interest expenses from borrowing money either through bonds, loans, convertible debt or any other lines of credit. Conversely, a company may also have interest income from investments. Like depreciation, this line item is considered a non-operating expense since again, it is outside of production (COGS and OPEX).

Since interest expense is usually greater than interest income, this term is usually referred to as *net interest expense*, or interest expense less any interest income in the period.

### Earning Before Tax (Pretax Income)

Almost home! Let's take a moment here to remember how far we've come. We started at the top line of the income statement (gross revenue), accounted for our industry take rate to arrive at net revenue, subtracted all costs of labor and raw materials (COGS) as well as the costs of production (OPEX), and accounted for non-operating expense items like D&A and interest. This leaves us at *pre-tax income*. All that remains is deducting the income tax.

## Income Tax

All companies pay some form of *income tax* and this line item represents an estimate of what they are expected to pay. Corporate income tax is about 39 percent although usually they'll use 40 percent in an interview. Here's a simple little trick to help you along and make you look smarter.[35]

If you have $300 and a 50 percent tax rate, you are at $150 net income. Easy. You probably did this intuitively but you can break it down into steps if the tax rate ends in "0".

Step I — Take your earnings before tax (EBT) and if the tax rate ends in "0", divide EBT by 10. In the above example this gives us 300 / 10 = 30.

Step II — Take the answer from Step I and multiply it by the first percentage digit of the tax rate to arrive at the income tax expense. 30 * 5 = 150.

If you gave me an EBT of $130 and a tax rate of 40 percent, I can instantly know that the *income tax* will be $52 dollars with the above trick. This means the net income, or what the business has earned after all expenses and taxes, is $78. Try it out a few times, commit it to memory if it helps you. This really saved me in quite a few interviews.

If the tax rate ends in "5", we'll have to add another half step, but the process is still relatively simple. Let's do 35 percent of $400 EBT.

Step I — Let's take our EBT of $400 and divide it by 10. 400 / 10 = 40.

Step Ib — Take Step I and divide by 2. 40 / 2 = 20.

Step II — Like the previous example. Take Step I and multiply by the first percentage digit, in this case, the "3". So, 40 x 3 = 120.

Step IIb — Add Step Ib and Step II. $120 + $20 = $140 income tax expense.

Step III — Subtract Step IIb from EBT to arrive at net income.

Slightly trickier, but keep practicing and I promise this trick will pay off in interviews and throughout your internship.

## Net Income

Finally, net income is considered the bottom line of the income statement. This line-item reveals the earnings of a company in a given period. Other names include net profit or net earnings.

Keep in mind that the income statement can be summed up as revenue minus expenses, so if expenses are larger than revenue we'll likely have a net loss here instead of net income.

Congratulations on making it through the income statement! Two more to go. I've outlined what a sample e-commerce company's P&L may look like in the next section. The information may appear less formal than we discussed, but it's important nonetheless to see how companies typically lay out their financials.

| Sample E-Commerce Company | |
|---|---|
| Orders (M) | 600 |
| Average Order Value (AOV) | 75 |
| Gross Transaction Value (GTV) | $45,000 |
| Take Rate | 15.0% |
| Net Revenue | $6,750 |
| COGS | 2,025 |
| Gross Profit | $4,725 |
| % Margin | %70.0 |
| | |
| **Operating Costs:** | |
| Operations and Support | 1,200 |
| Sales and Marketing | 2,400 |
| R&D | 535 |
| G&A | 450 |
| D&A | 335 |
| **Total Operation Costs** | $4,920 |
| | |
| Operating Profit | ($195) |

## Balance Sheet

The *balance sheet* is a snapshot in time of what a company owns and owes, in other words their financial position. Like the other financial statements, the balance sheet of a company can be seen on quarterly reports and annual reports.

The balance sheet helps an analyst or banker determine whether or not a company is worthy of additional credit or loans. As discussed in the venture debt chapter, a VC may look into an early stage company's balance sheet to determine how much debt they have. This adversely affects their inclination to move forward with an investment.

The balance sheet can be reduced to a simple equation that must always hold true:

$$Assets = Liabilities + Equity$$

We'll dive into the meaning of these terms now.

### Assets

*Assets* are what a company owns. They represent all sorts of items like machinery, land, factories, inventory, cash, *accounts receivable* (short-term money that a company is owed or will collect within one year) and anything else that can be expressed in dollars. For the purposes of breaking into venture capital, we'll need to know the definition and some examples of the line items listed above. If you wish for a more in-depth analysis, read Feldman or Tracy.

The balance sheet differentiates between a *long-term asset*, or an asset that is not fully consumed in one year like a factory or heavy machinery and *current assets* like cash and inventory that can indeed be consumed or liquidated in one year.

We'll also go over some sample questions later in the guide to test your knowledge.

### Liabilities

Just as an asset represents what a company owns, a *liability* represents what a company owes. When we talked about assets we mentioned the term accounts receivable. We used "receivable" because this represents money that a company is scheduled to receive within the year. Likewise, unless explicitly referenced as a long-term liability, most line items in liabilities have the term "payable" at the end to signify the company's obligation to pay within the year.

Here are some examples and definitions of liabilities:

*Accounts Payable* — Companies usually purchase goods and services on credit. Between the time they receive the good or service and the time they actually pay, the cost will be listed under accounts payable.

*Salaries Payable* — Employees earn a salary as they work, but aren't paid immediately. Before the company pays the salary of an employee, that amount of money will be accounted for under salaries payable.

*Interest Payable* — A company may owe interest, but not pay upfront. Interest payable represents their obligation to pay interest that is owed within the period.

*Current Liabilities* — These are obligations that are due within a given period. Since accounts, salaries and interest payable all must be paid within that particular year or quarter (depending on the statement), all of the above are considered current liabilities.

*Non-Current Liabilities* — Also known as long-term liabilities these are obligations that are not payable within a year and are usually summed up as long-term debt.

## Working Capital: A Simple Financial Metric

*Working Capital* — This refers to a company's ability to cover short-term liabilities. In order to benchmark this figure, we take current assets and subtract current liabilities.

Working Capital = Current Assets - Current Liabilities

## Equity

*Equity*, or shareholders' equity represents a source or claim on the company's assets. You may sometimes hear the term *book value* when a company is talking about equity. Book value is the reported assets of a company minus its liabilities. If we rearrange our accounting definition, we can see that this is the exact meaning of equity as well.

*Assets = Liabilities + Equity*

*Equity = Assets - Liabilities*

Let's work through a case study to get a better understanding of these terms.

A company has just had its IPO and wants to raise $20M so they decide to sell 1M shares at $20 to get $20M. But not every stock is sold at $20, some investors get a better deal and some don't. Regardless, the SEC and accounting bodies make every company's stock have a *par value*, which is the minimum or floor value of a stock, let's say it's 10 cents here. If the company sells 1,000,000 shares at a 10 cents par value per share, the total amount ($100,000) is recorded as the *common stock value*.

*Common Stock Value* — Par value (10 cents) * # of shares (1M). In our above example the common stock value is 10 cents * 1M shares = $100,000.

*Par Value* — As stated above, this is the number that sets the floor price of a stock. It's an arbitrary value and you can't sell any shares at a price below this amount.

*Preferred Stock* — Just like common stock but a high claim on assets and no voting rights. Although this term has great relevance in the venture capital world, it doesn't really play into VC interviews.

*Additional Paid-In Capital* — The price paid by the investor over the par value. Since we wanted to raise $20M and the common stock value is $100,000, the remaining portion is put in additional paid-in capital. This comes out to $19.9M.

*Treasury Stock* — Treasury stock represents a company's own shares that they bought back from the market. For instance, a company sells 1M shares to the market but now wants to buy 100 shares back. The company goes to the market and buys the stock at market price. Therefore, if the market price is $10 they need to have $1000 to buy 100 shares. Since cash is flowing out of the company to buy shares, the treasury stock is a negative account or a *contra-equity account*. For this reason, shareholders' equity itself goes down $1000 which alters cash on the asset side.

*Dividends* — You may have heard of this term before, dividends are just payments made to shareholders. If you own stock in a company and they issue a dividend, it means they will pay you either in cash or additional shares.

*Retained Earnings* — Retained earnings are your savings account in a way. It's where all the money ends up. Let's let RE = Retained earnings and I'll walk you through the simple version:

$$RE_{new} = RE_{original} + \text{Net Income} - \text{Dividends}$$

In order to find out the new retained earnings for a period, we start with the retained earnings from the last period, add our new net income and subtract any new dividends.

## Bookings vs. Revenue vs. Collections

There are terms commonly used in the software business that I will highlight here. If a Software-as-a-Service (SaaS) company provides a subscription agreement or contract to a customer, this counts as a *booking*. In other words, the customer has committing to spending money with the company, that is all. A contract is not necessarily required either. The customer could have simply signed up for the service on the company website.

The booking becomes *recognized revenue* and can be recorded as an accounts receivable once the SaaS company provides the service.

*Collections* are when money is collected from the customer. Now this can actually happen before services are rendered. For instance, if the software company collects the first six months of cash from a year-long subscription agreement immediately, although this is technically a collection it is also considered *deferred revenue*, or revenue that has yet to be accounted for and is therefore a liability. If the company were to go bankrupt tomorrow, the revenue collected from those six months would not be earned or recognized because services were not delivered.[36]

$$\text{Book-to-Bill Ratio} = \text{Bookings} / \text{Recognized Revenue}$$

Many companies use the *book-to-bill ratio* as a metric to make predictions on the cash flow and financial health of their business. If for every $1 of revenue the company has $1 in bookings or more, then the company is realizing revenue from customers fairly well and there is strong demand. If the company is having a hard time turning bookings into revenue (a book-to-bill ratio less than one) it can be said that the company is having a difficult time realizing revenue from customers or there is low demand.[37]

## Bookings vs. Revenue vs. Collections Example

To recap with a simple example: a customer signs a $12,000 year-long subscription agreement in January and pays the company quarterly. When that contract is signed, the company gets $12,000 in bookings. At the end of January, the company has rendered services for one month and can therefore count $1,000 as recognized revenue. However, there is still $11,000 of deferred revenue since services for the subsequent 11 months have not been delivered yet.

Although the company has earned revenue up to this point, they have not actually collected any cash on the agreement. Since the customer has agreed to pay every quarter, at the end of the first three months (March) the company will be able to account for $3,000 in collections.

## Cash Flow Statement

The *cash flow statement* allows us to know the flow of cash in a given period, also known as the cash inflow and cash outflow. The purpose of the cash flow statement is to see how cash is changing from one year to the next. The bottom line of this statement determines the change in cash, or net cash in a given period.

There are three buckets for all cash inflows and outflows, we'll discuss them below.

## Cash Flow from Operations (CFO)

I'll refer you to Feldman's *Accounting and Financial Statement Analysis* if you'd like to understand cash flow in more detail, but for interview purposes let's stick with the definition and key line items.

*Cash flow from operations (CFO)* indicates the cash brought in from ongoing core business activities like sales of goods or services. Here are some key line items:

*Net Income*—This is the same net income for the bottom of the income statement. It will serve as the first line item in CFO.

*Changes in Working Capital*—Since working capital is current assets minus current liabilities. Changes in working capital measures this difference across the periods.

If a company has cash inflows through long-term business activities, like the sale of a building or financial activity, like dividends, then these inflows will fall into some of the other cash flow buckets besides CFO.

A note here about depreciation in CFO. What is depreciation really? It's a theoretical way to measure decay or cost of an asset per period. Even though we subtracted depreciation in the income statement, there was never any real cash outflow in the period. It is for this reason that we *add depreciation back into CFO*. We'll discuss how this flows into VC interviews below, but for more on the cash flow statement read Feldman. A quick back-of-the-napkin way to get CFO is EBIT + Depreciation - Taxes.

## Cash Flow from Investing (CFI)

Intuitively you may think *cash flow from investing (CFI)* has to do with money from investing or maybe money invested into a company, but this isn't the definition. Cash flow from investing has to do with the buying and selling of long-term assets like buildings and heavy machinery, otherwise referred to as *property, plant and equipment (PP&E)*.

If you sell any property or heavy equipment, you'll likely have a positive number here because of the cash inflow. If you buy a new factory you'll likely have a negative number here, indicating a cash outflow.

## Cash Flow from Financing (CFF)

*Cash flow from financing (CFF)* is the flow of cash between the company and its creditors. Anything that has to do with raising money or repaying shareholders will fall into this bucket. What this means is if the company borrows money to meet any number of obligations, this will be considered a cash inflow in CFF. If the company has to issue cash dividends to its shareholders, this will be considered a cash outflow in CFF.

These are the basics of the cash flow statement for venture capital interview purposes. As you can imagine, they'd like you to understand what a cash flow statement is on a very high level and why each bucket matters, but you won't anguish over some of the more minute details that keep your investment banking friends up at night.

Regardless, if you'd like to know more I highly recommend Feldman's *Accounting and Financial Statement Analysis*. Matan runs an investment banking course called WallStreetPrep, so you'll know more than enough about financial statements for our purposes even after skimming Matan's book.

## What Do I Really Need to Know for Interviews?

We've covered a lot of financial information in this chapter. This is more of an overview so you don't go into a venture capital interview blind. Although these questions won't be the bulk of the interview, here are some standard questions you should be prepared for especially if you have any financial experience on your resume.

### Walk Me Through the Income Statement from Top to Bottom

*First we start at gross revenue — the top line. If we're dealing with a marketplace or e-commerce P&L, we'll note the company's take rate and account for net revenue. We'll then subtract COGS, the cost of goods sold to arrive at gross profit. From there we subtract OPEX, or operating expenses which contain our sales, general and administrative expenses (SG&A) as well as research and development costs (R&D).*

*This gets us down to EBITDA, or earnings before interest, tax, depreciation and amortization. From there we'll subtract depreciation and amortization to arrive at operating profit, or EBIT.*

*Finally we'll subtract net interest expense and income tax to arrive at net income or the bottom line of the income statement.*

### How Are These Statements Connected?

Think of the acronym ICB—"I C Billions" = Income Statement -> Cash Flow Statement -> Balance Sheet.

*On the income statement we go from revenue to the bottom line item, net income. That same net income figure is the first line item on the cash flow statement under cash flow from operations (CFO).*

*After accounting for all the cash inflows and outflows we'll get our change in cash, or net cash at the bottom of the cash flow statement.*

*We add that change in cash from the bottom of the cash flow statement to the cash line item from the previous period's balance sheet. So, if we want 2016 cash, we take 2015 cash from the balance sheet and add in the 2016 change in cash.*

*Finally, we can also say that the net income from the income statement flows into retained earnings on the shareholders' equity side of the balance sheet.*

*This connects the three statements but there are other minor links as well, like inventory that must be related to cost of goods sold.*

## How Does Depreciation Work? What Is the Depreciation If I Pay $1000 for a Computer?

*Depreciation allocates the cost of a physical asset over its lifetime. The most common way to account for it is through straight-line depreciation.*

*If the purchase price is $1000, I'd need a few more things to calculate depreciation. What is the salvage value and useful life of the asset?*

($500 salvage value and 10-year lifetime)

*If the salvage value is $500 and the asset has a 10-year useful life then we'll depreciate $50 per year for the next 10 years.*

## How Does a $10 Depreciation Expense Affect the Three Financial Statements?

(This is a really good one to know!)

*I'll start with the income statement. Nothing above EBITDA will change since depreciation is a non-operating expense. After EBITDA we'll subtract $10 for the depreciation expense to get to EBIT.*

*I'll assume no interest here and move onto the tax rate, which I'll estimate to be 40 percent. (1-tax rate) multiplied* *by depreciation will leave us with a $6 expense, or a net loss of $6 for the period.*

*That same $6 net loss will be the first line item on the cash flow statement under CFO. Since depreciation doesn't explicitly involve any cash inflow or outflow, we'll add it back in cash flow from operations (CFO). All else being equal, we'll have a change in cash of $4 for the period (-$6 + $10 = $4).*

*We'll add that $4 in new cash to the balance sheet under assets but we also need to account for the depreciation expense here as well so we'll subtract $10 from assets here, leaving the company with -$6 on the asset side.*

*Finally, we'll add our net loss of $6 to the retained earnings under shareholders' equity and now since assets are at -$6 and liabilities (no change) and equity together are at -$6, our balance sheet is balanced.*

### Rapid-Fire Questions

Be able to answer these rapid-fire questions, preferably in one or two sentences.

### Income Statement Rapid Questions

Q. What's an income statement?

A. An income statement is a financial statement that starts from the revenue line, takes out expenses and reaches net income.

Q. What kinds of expenses are you taking out?

A. Well, there's COGS, SG&A and R&D.

Q. What does OPEX cover?

A. OPEX covers SG&A and R&D.

Q. What do you get after subtracting this?

A. You get EBITDA.

Q. What's EBTIDA?

A. Well EBTIDA stands for earnings before interest, taxes, depreciation and amortization.

Q. What's depreciation?

A. Depreciation is dividing the cost of a physical asset throughout the years of its use.

Q. What's the formula for depreciation?

A. (Purchase Price - Salvage Value) / Useful Life of the Asset.

Q. Well let's do a depreciation example. We bought something for $1000, what's the depreciation?

A. To calculate that I'm going to need to know how much we'll sell it for.

(Okay, we'll sell it for 500 bucks)

And what is the useful life of the asset?

(Oh, it's five years)

Depreciation is 100 dollars.

## Balance Sheet Rapid Questions

Q. What is a balance sheet?

A. A balance sheet is snapshot in time showing what a company owns and what it owes.

Q. What are the sections of a balance sheet?

A. Assets, liabilities and shareholders' equity.

Q. What type of assets are there?

A. Long-term and short-term.

Q. What are the types of current or short-term assets?

A. Cash, accounts receivable and inventory generally.

Q. What are some of the long-term liabilities?

A. Usually long-term debt.

Q. What is shareholders' equity?

A. A firm's assets minus its liabilities.

Q. How many components does it have?

A. It has several components: common stock, treasury stock, additional paid-in capital, retained earnings and dividends.

Q. What's treasury stock?

A. It's a negative account. It's whenever companies buy back their own stock from the market.

Q. How do you calculate retained earnings?

A. Your original retained earnings from the beginning of the period plus net income from the current period minus any dividends from the current period.

Q. What is difference between bookings, revenue and collections?

A. A booking is when a customer agrees to spend money, revenue is recognized when services are rendered and collections are simply when the customer's cash hits the company bank account.

Q. Can collections occur before revenue is recognized?

A. Sure. If this happens the revenue is considered deferred revenue, which is a liability.

## Cash Flow Rapid Questions

Q. What is the cash flow statement?

A. It looks at how the cash account changes from one year to the next.

Q. Where does the new cash flow line item go?

A. Next year's balance sheet.

Q. What is the first line item?

A. Net income.

Q. What are the three sections?

A. Cash flow from operations (CFO), cash flow from financing (CFF) and cash flow from investing (CFI).

Q. What's in operations?

A. Net income, adjustments for non-cash items like depreciation, then changes in working capital.

Q. Why adjust for non-cash items?

A. Because they are virtual line items and since they impact the net income in a virtual way, you need to account for that.

Chapter 12
# RETURNS AND VALUATION
*WHAT YOU NEED TO KNOW*

## Returns

A venture capitalist is expecting a certain return over a time horizon when they invest in a company. Over a 5-year investment time horizon, investors typically anticipate a 20-30 percent *internal rate of return (IRR)* which lands anywhere between 2.5-4.0x, or "two and a half to four times" the original money invested. The internal rate of return is an annualized growth rate that accounts for cash inflows and outflows within the period.

Compared to simply compounding the annual growth rate of an investment, IRR is considered a better way to measure profitability over time expressly because it accounts for all cashflows, or in other words makes the *net present value (NPV)* of all cash inflows and outflows equal to zero.

While it is difficult and unnecessary to know how to calculate IRR in an interview given the proper inputs, there are a few quick numbers you can memorize and put to use that may benefit you greatly in an interview.

If ever IRR is discussed in an interview, investors are usually referring to a 5-year time horizon. The chart below is a standard IRR table which tells us the return multiples for a given IRR as long as we know the years invested.[38]

**ROI on Invested Capital**

|  | 1.5x | 2x | 3x | 4x | 5x | 6x |
|---|---|---|---|---|---|---|
| **2** | 22% | 41% | 73% | 100% | 124% | 145% |
| **3** | 14% | 26% | 44% | 59% | 71% | 82% |
| **4** | 11% | 19% | 32% | 41% | 50% | 57% |
| **5** | 8% | 15% | 25% | 32% | 38% | 43% |
| **6** | 7% | 12% | 20% | 26% | 31% | 35% |
| **7** | 6% | 10% | 17% | 22% | 26% | 29% |
| **8** | 5% | 9% | 15% | 19% | 22% | 25% |
| **9** | 5% | 8% | 13% | 17% | 20% | 22% |
| **10** | 4% | 7% | 12% | 15% | 17% | 20% |

*Years Invested* (row axis label)

The shaded green cells represent the IRRs that are at or above the desired return given the years invested. If we want 4 times our investment in 5 years we need about a 30 percent IRR.

These questions are common in private equity interviews and may arise in venture capital interviews as well, however they will usually associate with a 5-year time horizon.

When an interviewer discusses IRR over a 5-year period, they may associate a 1.5x return with ~10 percent IRR, 2x with 15 percent IRR, 3x with 25 percent IRR, 4x with ~30 percent IRR, 5x with 40 percent IRR and 6x with 45 percent IRR. Given any amount invested and any IRR, we can now easily find the money returned or ROI. We'll take a closer look during the rapid-fire questions.

## Valuation

*Valuation* is described as an art and a science. The goal here is to use several different methods to get a range, or *football field* of values that will tell us what a given company is worth.

I'll give a cursory overview of how to interpret startup valuations as well as walk through several valuation techniques that you will likely encounter at a high level with venture associates or vice presidents.

## Pre-Money and Post-Money Valuation

Before we dive into pre- and post-money valuation let's define "money" as the amount of venture capital invested in a round of financing. Now we can understand *post-money valuation* as the value of a company, immediately after the latest amount of venture capital is invested.

Therefore, *pre-money valuation* is the value of a company before that latest round of capital has been invested. This is typically the value of the idea, opportunity, the management team and perhaps any patents or intellectual property that comes with the founders. Distilling our understanding of pre- and post-money valuation, it must be that:

Post-Money Valuation = Pre-Money Valuation + Amount Invested
Pre-Money Valuation = Post Money Valuation − Amount Invested

Key differences between the two are the timing of the valuation and ownership stake.

**Pre-Money Valuation**

|  | Value | Percent |
|---|---|---|
| Entrepreneur | $100 | 80% |
| Investor | $25 | 20% |
| Total | $125 | 100% |

**Post-Money Valuation**

|  | Value | Percent |
|---|---|---|
| Entrepreneur | $75 | 75% |
| Investor | $25 | 25% |
| Total | $100 | 100% |

## Ownership Stake

Let's say the entrepreneur and the investor agree that a company is worth $100 and we are willing to put in $25. As the table below indicates, our equity stake as VCs is dependent upon whether the valuation was pre-money or post-money.

At a pre-money valuation of $100 (the entrepreneur's line item), an investment of $25 is proportionally smaller relative to the total capital and so investors get a smaller piece of the pie (20 percent). At a post-money valuation of $100 (total capital), a $25 investment is already built into the value and thus represents a relatively larger piece of the pie (25 percent).

All else being equal, if the pre- and post-money valuations are the same amount and the amount invested is the same, we can assume that the entrepreneur has relatively less equity and the venture capitalist has relatively more equity in the post-money valuation.[39]

## In an Interview

In a venture capital interview, they may have a few sentences written down describing a pre-money or post-money valuation, and have you fill in the percentages or ask you a similar question point blank.

The idea here is to test your understanding of terms on a fundamental level so the arithmetic will remain relatively simple. That being said, there's a simple trick here that can benefit you.

The pre- and post-money valuation amount will likely be the same as will the amount invested. The amount invested in the pre-money example will likely represent 1/5th or 1/4th of the total (20 percent or 25 percent), but could also represent 1/3rd or 1/2 of the total (33 percent or 50 percent).

In the simple universe of these interview examples, let $n_{pre}$ equal the number of times the investment amount in a pre-money example can factor into the pre-money valuation—any whole number from 2 to 5—where $1/n_{pre}$ equals the proportion of the company that the investor owns after adding the investment amount to the pre-money valuation (e.g. 1/5 means 20 percent investor ownership etc.).

All else being equal, the same amount invested in the post-money valuation example represents a greater proportion of investor ownership. If the pre- and post-money valuations are the same in a given question and the amount invested is the same as well, you can think of investor ownership in the post-money valuation example as $1/(n_{pre}-1)$.

If the pre-money investment represents 20 percent of the total or 1/5th, the post-money investment should represent 25 percent or 1/4th of the total.

For instance, if we invest $250k at a pre-money valuation of $1M this gives the company $1.25M in total capital and we get 20 percent ownership as investors. As a post-money question, if we invested $250k at a post-money valuation of $1M we own 25 percent of the company.

Alternatively, if we invest $500k at a pre-money valuation of $1M, the company now has $1.5M in total capital and we as investors own ~33.3 percent or 1/3rd of the company. If asked as a post-money question with the same investment amount, the post-money valuation is $1M and the $500k investment now represents 50 percent investor ownership of the company. Huge difference.

These are fundamental questions that may be posed very early in the interview, so try to create quick little pre- and post-money valuation questions to ace this part of the process!

Here is a quick table to summarize, where "Pre" represents the investment amount as a proportion of the pre-money valuation and "Post" represents the investment amount as a proportion of the post-money valuation. In the table below any pre-money investment amount represents 1/n of the total committed capital or *paid-in capital (PIC)*. That same investment considered in a post-money valuation scenario makes up $1/(n_{pre}-1)$ of the total committed capital.

| Pre | Post |
|-----|------|
| 20% | 25% |
| 25% | 33% |
| 33% | 50% |
| 50% | 100% |

## Where Is the Value?

When a venture capital firm invests in a startup, the value is realized through the private shares that the firm now owns after investing. In an overly simplified example, a company may have a pre-money valuation of $2M and a VC firm invests $500k (so the post-money valuation is $2.5M and the investor owns 20 percent of the business).

The value of that $500k investment is realized in private shares. If each share is $1 than the VC firm has 500k shares while the company still holds the majority at 2M shares.

## Primary and Secondary Shares

A quick note on primary and secondary. These $1 shares are considered *primary shares* if they were issued for the investors in this round and have no prior owner. If the $1 shares had a prior owner, like an early angel investor or founder who wants to cash out, these are considered *secondary shares* since two individuals are simply trading shares amongst themselves. The main idea here is primary shares represent the creation of value while secondary shares instead imply the trading of value between investors and entrepreneurs.

## Enterprise Value

Before getting into valuation techniques, let's understand the concept of *enterprise value*. This is the number we are looking for, or the answer to the question "How much should I pay for this company?" Enterprise value is the value of the entire firm.

## Calculating Enterprise Value

Although enterprise value typically deals with public companies, some late stage venture capital firms may want interns and new hires to understand the internal dynamics of valuation more thoroughly. The equation for enterprise value is below.

Enterprise Value = Equity Value + Debt – Cash + Minority Interest

## Equity

In the context of enterprise value, *equity* is just the total value of a company's stock, otherwise known as the market capitalization of a company. Simply multiply the price of the stock (let's say it's $9) by the number of shares issued (100).

In this example the equity value, or market capitalization is $9 * 100 shares or $900.

## Debt

*Debt* represents what a company owes. Here, we can find all debt from the balance sheet. We'll total short-term and long-term debt to arrive at this number.

## Cash

If you buy a house for $100, but the house comes with $5 cash inside, you actually only paid $95 (or $100 - $5). Since a company's *cash* on hand can be easily deployed by the new buyer after the purchase, cash is subtracted in the equation. 99 percent of the time all you need to know is equity, debt and cash in an interview.

## Minority Interest

Whenever a parent company owns more than 50 percent of a subsidiary company, that parent company needs to represent 100 percent of the subsidiary's assets, liabilities and equity on its financial statements. The parent company's balance sheet will have a line item that says *minority interest*. This represents the equity of the subsidiary company that the parent company does not own.

If we bought 80 percent of a company, the remaining 20 percent of equity is considered minority interest and can be found on the minority interest line item on the balance sheet. This is the figure we put down in the enterprise value equation.

### Discounted Cash Flow (DCF)

DCF stands for *discounted cash flow*, a technique where you take all the money that a company is estimated to make in the foreseeable future (usually five years), and convert those "future dollars" to "present day" dollars. In an interview you can refer to this as "discounting the value of all future cash flows to arrive at the *present value* of a company." Since startups lack much of the fundamentals needed for the DCF approach, any question related to discounted cash flow is likely to only appear qualitatively in a growth equity interview.

There are many investment banking guides that outline the entire DCF valuation process from start to finish. However, in a late stage venture capital interview they will only ask for a big picture understanding, so I'll only focus on the overview. First let's highlight key terms and then answer some basic valuation questions.

### Free Cash Flow (FCF)

*Free cash flow* is the "spending money" of a company, or the money that is left over after all core expenses are paid. Since—ideally, free cash flow will be generated every year, this amount represents the "future dollars" that will be discounted to "present day" dollars in order to value the company.

Free cash flow is also a metric to keep track of profitability. Positive free cash flow means a company is generating a solid profit. If the free cash flow is negative, it usually signifies that a company cannot cover operations solely from running the business. In the universe of early and growth stage technology companies, most business have not generated positive cash flow and therefore require venture capital in order to grow the business.

## Discount Rate (WACC)

Remember, we need to discount the "future dollars" to arrive at a present value of the company. The *discount rate* we use is an average of what the company is paying for debt (interest) and what they are paying for equity.

This discount rate is aptly called the *weighted average cost of capital (WACC)*. Since equity and debt holders are foregoing the next best investment here, think of WACC as the return that equity owners and lenders expect from a company. If we're talking about public or private middle-market companies, the WACC (expected return) will be much smaller because the risk profile is much lower for companies of that size, I'll show you how WACC changes in venture capital scenarios further in this section. For the sake of our example here, let's assume WACC is 10 percent. We will discount every year's free cash flow by (1 + WACC) in the form of:

$$\frac{FCF_t}{(1 + WACC)^t}$$

Five years of discounted cash flow becomes:

$$PV = \frac{FCF_1}{(1 + WACC)} + \frac{FCF_2}{(1 + WACC)^2} + \frac{FCF_3}{(1 + WACC)^3} + \frac{FCF_4}{(1 + WACC)^4} + \frac{FCF_5 \times (1 + g)}{(WACC - g)}$$

## Present Value

Since we've successfully discounted all future cash flows, the "PV" above does indeed stand for *present value*, or in other words the value of the company using the discounted cash flow method.

## Terminal Value

One of these things is not like the other. You'll notice that the last free cash flow, $FCF_5$ is multiplied by a "1+g" and divided by a "WACC-g". This "g" signifies the rate at which the cash flows of the company are expected to grow forever. Otherwise known as the perpetuity growth rate, this number can be found in analyst reports and is typically between 2-4 percent.[40]

If we have a big number like $FCF_5$ x (1 + g * (2 percent)) and we divide by a really small number WACC (10 percent) – g * (2 percent), we will get a really big number—*terminal value*, or the extended value of the company beyond five years. In general, it is improbable to forecast beyond five years due to macroeconomic uncertainty.

### DCF Use Case in Venture Capital

Above is the formal way to understand DCF analysis. When the method is implemented in venture capital we need to tweak some of the parameters like WACC, the weighted average cost of capital. While 10 percent was an ample return for middle market and public companies, venture investors need a much higher return because the companies have a much larger risk profile.

It is the same analysis and same formula as above, except we will use a higher discount rate to adjust for the larger risk. The earlier we go, the higher the risk profile. An early stage firm may target a 60 percent IRR (~10x ROI). If so, they would use a 60 percent WACC to discount all future cash flows.[41]

### Walking Through a DCF

Now, investment banking interviewers will approach this question a lot differently than venture capitalists.

If this were a banking interview guide I would lay out the formulas and walk through how to find each variable in the discounted cash flow valuation method, but it's not. In an interview setting we can summarize the DCF process by saying:

> In a DCF analysis we would discount the value of all future cash flows by the weighted average cost of capital and add the terminal year value to arrive at the present value of our company.

If asked this question you likely have some finance experience on your resume, but it still makes sense to understand this approach fundamentally as you prepare for venture capital interviews.

### Comparables

*Comparable company analysis*, or "comps" is another way to value our target company. We are creating a universe of several sample companies here that all have one thing in common. Whether that be location, product, capital structure or anything else is entirely up to you (this is where the art comes in).

Comps allows you to quickly and easily value the target company without diving deeper into their financials. It serves as a gut check for some of the more in-depth techniques like DCF. The method only requires two components.

## Enterprise Value

The enterprise value will likely be readily available, but you can also calculate it using the formula mentioned above (EV = Equity Value + Debt - Cash + Minority Interest).

## EBITDA

As referenced in the accounting chapter, EBITDA stands for earnings before interest, taxes, depreciation and amortization. I will use EBITDA here to create a ratio that helps determine the value of a company. Analysts use EBITDA instead of net income because companies tend to have different tax structures, financing costs and even methods of depreciation.

A common saying is EBITDA allows us to compare "apples to apples," whereas using net income would essentially compare "apples to oranges."

## The Multiple: How to Calculate (EV/EBITDA)

After dividing a company's enterprise value by its EBITDA we'll arrive at a multiple like 5x (read as "five times"). 5x means that the market values this particular company at 5 times its earnings, in other words the market values every $1 this company makes as if it were $5.

If a sample company has an enterprise value of $100 and an EBITDA of $20, the company's multiple (EV/EBITDA) is 5x.

## Walking Through Comparables

We can't just compare our target company with one sample company. In order to successfully perform a comparable companies analysis we need multiple sample companies. Ideally we want at least three companies in our sample so we can get a range consisting of a minimum, maximum and average value.

If Microsoft is valued at 7x, Amazon is valued at 8x and Google is valued at 9x, those values will give us our minimum, average, and maximum, respectively and we'll use the average multiple for our comps analysis, 8x in this case.

We arrive at our comparable companies valuation once we multiply the sample average multiple (8x) by our target EBITDA. For instance, if our target EBITDA is $10 then our comps valuation will be $80.

## Use Cases in Venture Capital

As mentioned earlier, cash flow is usually negative for early and growth stage technology companies so as a result these are largely EBITDA-negative businesses. How do we calculate an enterprise value for a business like this? Well, in venture we'll use sales as a proxy for EBITDA to create the EV/sales multiple.

Instead of looking at the EBITDA of sample companies, we'll simply look at the top line of their income statements to get revenue, or net revenue if valuing an e-commerce or marketplace business.

## Precedent Transactions Analysis

*Precedent transactions analysis (PTA)* is very similar to comps and uses the same multiples. The only difference is this valuation technique is focused on transactions that actually occurred, as opposed to a sample of similar companies.

Since firms are usually sold at a premium to what they are inherently worth—often called a *control premium*—the valuation in PTA will tend to be larger.

Additionally, PTA has the added restriction of time frame. You don't want to go back more than five years as that particular transaction may not reflect current market conditions.

## EBITDA and Enterprise Value Under PTA

We'll use EBITDA and enterprise value of the target company at the time it was purchased.

## Walking Through PTA

Similar to comps, a precedent transactions analysis only becomes useful when we have at least three past deals to create a minimum, average and maximum value. Like comps, we will use the average multiple and multiply by the target EBITDA to arrive at the precedent transactions analysis valuation. Since early and growth stage companies tend to be EBITDA-negative, we will use sales as a proxy for EBITDA to generate an EV/sales multiple whenever possible.

## Asset-Based Valuation

Recall from the financial statements chapter that assets = liabilities + shareholders' equity. The *asset-based valuation* method is typically used when a company has no cash flow, is near bankruptcy and preparing to liquidate assets for sale. Asset-based valuation also comes in handy when a company's value can be largely derived from its tangible and intangible assets.

At a high level, we are assigning value to all assets (inventory, patents, accounts receivable) and all liabilities (accounts payable) on the balance sheet. Next, we simply rearrange the above accounting equation to solve for assets - liabilities.

Assets                       =    Liabilities + Shareholders' Equity
Assets – Liabilities   =    Asset-based Valuation Method

## Black-Scholes Model

This one is out of left field. If you mention the *Black-Scholes* model, interviewers will likely be impressed but won't expect you to walk through it. In 1973 two gentleman, Fischer Black and Myron Scholes published a paper titled *The Pricing of Options and Corporate Liabilities* and as the title suggests, this was a new way to price an option over time.[42]

## How to Talk About This

It is possible to value a company as an option using the Black-Scholes model but it is not used practically in the industry. However, taking the time to mention the analysis in an interview will show that you have a deep interest in finance, which always works in your favor.

## The Venture Capital Method

The *venture capital method* is not a definitive way to value a company, but rather a back of the napkin approach that VCs and angels can use to back out a valuation for an early stage company.

We determine what we think the company will be worth at exit through market conditions and industry multiples, then divide this number by the anticipated *return on investment (ROI)*, or the cash-on-cash return investors receive at exit as a multiple of what they originally invested (e.g. 10x etc.). The method is typically used for very early stage companies and emerged from a Harvard Business School case study published in 1987 by Professor William Sahlman.[43, 44]

### Enterprise Value and Multiples in the VC Method

There's some guesswork in this method, but it's rooted by experienced investors who have been investing in early stage companies for over 20 years. All we're doing here is finding the average EV/sales multiple for the industry sector of our target company.

First, we'll need to estimate the target's revenue in the nth year, or exit year. If we look at the universe of similar companies (possibly from a previous comps or precedent transactions analysis), we can determine median revenue in the exit year and attribute it to our target company, let's say it's $30M.

Now we need to find out what similar companies sold for as a multiple of their revenue. We can find the revenue and enterprise value of these similar transactions and use this data as a proxy, but it's most ideal to use banker's reports whenever available.

If our VC firm were approached by an early stage healthcare IT company—let's call it *Syntax Health*—asking for $500k, it may be best to use a report to better understand how the market is responding to the sector. A Berkery Noyes report from 2016 indicates that the average revenue multiple for HCIT companies is 2.8x.[45]

With $30M in revenue and an average revenue multiple of 2.8x, we can give our early stage healthcare company an enterprise value of $84M in its nth year, otherwise referred to as the *harvest year*, or exit year.

### Anticipated ROI in the VC Method

As discussed earlier, ROIs are cash-on-cash multiples of the money VCs or angels originally invested. Since the method skews towards very early stage companies, the anticipated ROIs are much higher because there is more risk towards the beginning of the business. An anticipated seed stage ROI is typically in the ballpark of 30x, compared to maybe 5-7x at the growth stage. I'll talk about why the ROI is so large towards the end of the section.

## Using the VC Method

Now that we have an enterprise value at an exit of $84M and a target ROI at an exit of 30x, we can use our formula.

$$\text{Post-Money Valuation} =$$
$$\text{Enterprise Value in the nth Year / Anticipated ROI in the nth Year} =$$
$$\$84M / 30x$$
$$\text{Post-Money Valuation} = \$2.8M$$

Now that we have the post-money valuation and know the investment amount, we can arrive at a pre-money valuation for our health care startup.

$$\text{Post-Money Valuation} = \text{Pre-Money Valuation} + \text{Amount Invested}$$
$$\text{Pre-Money Valuation} = \text{Post Money Valuation} - \text{Amount Invested}$$

Since our healthcare startup, Syntax Health is asking for an investment of $500k this gives them a pre-money valuation of $2.2M.

$$\text{Pre-Money Valuation} =$$
$$\$2.8M - \$500k = \$2.2M$$

While there's no generally accepted method of valuing startups that are early stage and likely pre-revenue, the venture capital method serves as a reference point to value startups at their earliest stage. Our example above indicates a deal size of $500k and a post-money valuation of $2.8M, giving the investor about 18 percent of the company.

Jeffrey Sohl, the director at the Center for Venture Research has been tracking the angel investor market for over 35 years. Data from his 2015 report shows that the average angel deal size in 2015 was $345,390 with an average post-money valuation of $2.32M, this means angels were typically getting about a 15 percent stake in early stage companies.[46]

Early stage investments have been in this range for the past decade or so. Our example wasn't too far off!

## Valuation Divergence at the Early Stage

If we invested $500k in Syntax Health, gaining about 18 percent of the company at a $2.8M post-money valuation and they indeed sold the venture for $84M, did we really just make 30x our money and exit with $15M dollars?

The reality of situation is that as the valuation of a company increases, the value of the private shares (your investment money) does not increase proportionately. Luis Villalobos, founder at Tech Coast Angels refers to this as *valuation divergence*: as a venture's valuation increases, its shares increase at a much lower rate.

Early stage investors will experience a cash-on-cash ROI decrease of as much as 3-5x. So, as early stage investors we won't receive $15M on the Syntax Health deal, we'll likely make somewhere between $3M and $5M or 6-10x our original investment.[47]

Due to the fund economics of early stage investing it may not make sense to do a *pro-rata*, or follow-on investment with a $5M Series A in order to maintain our 20 percent. As the entrepreneur continues to raise capital, the early stage investors will continue to experience a valuation dilution or divergence in their investor shares, effectively changing their ROI from investment to exit. The 30x ROI that early stage investors are gunning for actually doesn't account for valuation divergence; the real ROI is something like 5-10x.[48]

Here's a quick look at an early stage IRR table to see where angels and early stage investors need to target returns. We can see that the returns are much higher than what is typical at the growth stage because the risk profile of early stage investing is much higher as well.[49]

**Sweet Spot**
**5-10x in 4-8 Years**

**ROI on Invested Capital**

|   |   | 5x | 6x | 7x | 8x | 9x | 10x |
|---|---|-----|-----|-----|-----|-----|-----|
| | 4 | 50% | 57% | 64% | 68% | 73% | 78% |
| | 5 | 38% | 43% | 48% | 52% | 55% | 58% |
| Years Invested | 6 | 31% | 35% | 38% | 41% | 44% | 47% |
| | 7 | 26% | 29% | 32% | 35% | 37% | 39% |
| | 8 | 22% | 25% | 28% | 30% | 32% | 33% |

**IRR Between 25-75%**

Angels typically aim for IRRs between 25 to 75 percent over a period of 4-8 years, this yields an ROI in the ballpark of 5-10x the invested capital and accounts for any valuation divergence across the period.

## Pre-Revenue Valuation Methods

Now that we've reviewed some of the more well-known methods of valuation, let's dive into a few other methods mostly used in the early stage to arrive at a pre-money valuation for pre-revenue companies.[50]

## Chicago Method

This is really just a small tweak in the discounted cash flow analysis. As you may have guessed in our venture capital DCF example, we are assuming close to a 10x return on our portfolio company in five years with a 60 percent WACC, possible but not the most likely scenario.

The *Chicago Method* uses three scenarios (success, sideways and failure) and estimates the probability of each in order to get a better idea of the potential enterprise value of a company. Since the idea is to smooth out risk with the three different scenarios, the Chicago Method also tends to use a much lower rate of return. Something like 40 percent IRR in five years (~5x) replaces the previous IRR, which also gives us a WACC of 40 percent as well. Here's an example in the form of a small chart.

|  | Success | Sideways | Failure |
|---|---|---|---|
| Probability | 10% | 30% | 60% |
| DCF | $40,000,000 | $3,000,000 | $500,000 |

We weight the value of each DCF scenario as follows to arrive at a $5.2M valuation.

$$10\% \times \$40M + 30\% \times \$3M + 60\% \times \$500k = \$5.2M$$

## Berkus Method

The *Berkus Method* is named after Dave Berkus, one of the most famous angels in early stage technology investing with over 130 investments. Dave cites that most early stage valuation techniques rely on the financial projections of the entrepreneur and in reality, only 1 in every 20 exceed those expectations. In the mid-90s he began to use his own insights and experience to come up with the following:[51]

| If Exists: | Add to Company Value: |
|---|---|
| 1. Sound Idea (basic value, product risk) | $500k |
| 2. Prototype (reducing technology risk) | $500k |
| 3. Quality Management Team (reducing execution risk) | $500k |
| 4. Strategic Relationships (reducing market risk and competitive risk) | $500k |
| 5. Product Rollout or Sales (reducing financial or production risk | $500k |

The Berkus valuation method can be adapted to almost any pre-revenue business. The method yields a maximum pre-money valuation of $2.5M, but only $2M for a pre-revenue business as the company could likely not add value in category 5 (existence of sales). Angel investors can value the business anywhere from zero to the $2.5M cap in accordance with how well they think the startup performs in a given test area.

Berkus states that pre-money valuations for pre-revenue businesses must be capped due to the inherent risk that angels take so early in the company lifecycle. Even if a company shows promise, it needs to be able to grow into its valuation and have the opportunity to achieve 8-10x its original value (factoring in valuation divergence over its lifetime). After a company begins earning revenue, the Berkus Method is no longer applicable.

## Risk Factor Summation Method

Some early stage investors consider the Berkus Method too narrow and require a much wider spectrum in order to evaluate pre-revenue startups. The *risk factor summation method*—as the name suggests—focuses on the overall risk profile of a company using a broader set of factors and a median pre-revenue valuation that is region-specific. The risk factor summation method maps out the following 12 risks.

1. Management

2. Stage of the business

3. Legislation/political risk

4. Manufacturing risk

5. Sales and marketing risk

6. Funding/capital raising risk

7. Competition risk

8. Technology risk

9. Litigation risk

10. International risk

11. Reputation risk

12. Potential lucrative exit

Each of the above risks is assessed as follows:

+2 Very positive for growing the company and executing a wonderful exit

+1 Positive

 0 Neutral

-1 Negative

-2 Very negative

The method then uses the average pre-revenue valuation of a particular region and the given sector if applicable, to establish a base pre-money valuation, which is then incremented by $250k for every +1 and decremented $250k for every -1. In the event of a +2 or -2, the valuation goes up or down $500k, respectively.

Bill Payne, a noted angel investor with over 30 years of experience, tracked pre-revenue valuations by surveying North American angel groups. He stopped publicly tracking in 2011, but surveyed 30 angel groups across the country and observed an average pre-money valuation of about $2M with not too much variance between regions.[52]

We can use Director of the Center for Venture Research, Jeffrey Sohl's 2015 data to arrive at an average pre-money valuation of $2M for pre-revenue deals.[53]

Assuming an average pre-money valuation for a pre-revenue company in the ballpark of $2M, if you add up all 12 risk factors and get three zeros, five +1's, one -1, one +2 and two -2's, then we have a net increment of +2 or $500k. Adding the increment to the base region valuation will give the company's pre-money valuation.

Add $500k to the average pre-money valuation of $2M to arrive at a $2.5M pre-money valuation for the given pre-revenue company using the risk factor summation method. Like most pre-revenue valuation methods, once the company is earning revenue the risk factor summation method is not applicable.

## Rule of Thirds

The *rule of thirds* is a straightforward rule of thumb that gives pre-revenue investors a third of the company, leaving another third for founders and the remaining third for future C-level executives and management. In other words if $800k is raised, the post-money valuation is $2.4M. If $1M is raised, the post-money valuation is $3M.

The thinking here is anyone willing to take risk on a pre-revenue company deserves a third of the company. A big caveat here—as seen above—is that every dollar raised triples the valuation, effectively incentivizing entrepreneurs to raise as much money as possible to get the highest valuation. The rule of thirds has since become more of a screening tactic than a valuation method.

If an entrepreneur is raising $250k and will not accept a $750k post-money valuation (in other words a $500k pre-money valuation), the deal may be too small from an equity and valuation standpoint for the investor. If the entrepreneur requires $1.5M and the angels will not accept a $4.5M post-money valuation ($3M pre-money valuation), the deal may be too large. As we saw with Jeffrey Sohl's work at the Center for Venture Research, somewhere around $2M is considered an actionable pre-money valuation for pre-revenue companies.

## Standard Value

I'll close this pre-revenue valuation subsection with the *standard value method*. We've seen a variety of ways to value pre-revenue companies and the pre-money valuations are usually in the ballpark of $2M-$3M. This is based on the expertise of seasoned pre-revenue investors like Bill Payne and Dave Berkus as well as venture research experts like Jeffrey Sohl.

Although some of these experts have developed their own method, the standard value method simply demarcates a pre-money valuation between $2M and $3M for pre-revenue companies no matter the business or industry.

Again, more of a screening model or preference for pre-revenue investors, but this is typically the valuation sweet spot for pre-revenue investors to achieve an 8-10x ROI upon a successful exit.[54]

This subsection serves as a primer for valuing pre-revenue companies and in no way attempts to outline every valuation method. For a more exhaustive summary of pre-revenue valuation methods check out the National Angel Organization's *Age of the Angel: Best Practice for Angel Groups and Investors*.[55]

## The Football Field

Valuation methodologies become more useful in aggregate. Firms create a singular graph detailing the range of each valuation in order to arrive at a proper final value that intersects all or most of the valuation techniques used; this graph is called a *football field*.

Remember that valuation is an art as well as a science. Looking back to the precedent transactions and comparable companies analyses, we used the average multiple but could just have easily gone with the highest or lowest multiple to create best and worst case scenarios. Likewise, with the discounted cash flow method we could adjust the growth rate or discount rate to create even more scenarios. For the venture capital method we could have also adjusted anticipated ROI in the exit year to arrive at an array of values.

Overall, this gives each valuation method a range of data as opposed to a single point on the graph below.

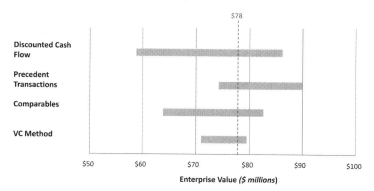

The data above is fictionalized, but for reference we used four valuation methodologies (DCF, comps, PTA and the VC method) to arrive at an average valuation of $78M.

It is just as common for the horizontal axis to represent share price. To back out an enterprise value when given share price, we would multiple the average share price by the number of private shares (remember—new private shares are issued every time a company raises a round, giving the company a higher valuation) to arrive at an equity value. From this point, we can add the anticipated debt and subtract the anticipated cash to arrive at the enterprise value.

## Rapid-Fire Questions

Q. What is more expensive: debt or equity?

A. Equity is more expensive because there is no ceiling on a company's profits and with debt, interest is fixed at something like 6 percent or 7 percent.

Q. How many shares outstanding of a company are there if the equity value is $1000?

A. I would need the share price.

(Share price is $50)

If the share price is $50 then there are 20 shares outstanding.

Q. If a company has an enterprise value of $500, $100 in debt, $200 in cash and no minority interest, what is the equity value?

A. We will subtract the debt from both sides and add cash to both sides to get an equity value of $600.

Q. Why do we subtract cash in the enterprise value equation?

A. Because it's cash on hand so we can use it however we see fit after purchasing a company. In this way, the cash on hand is considered a discount from the "purchase price" or enterprise value.

Q. What is a DCF, what are its pros and cons?

A. DCF stands for discounted cash flow analysis. We discount the value of all future cash flows in order to arrive at a present value of the target company. Some pros are that it uses most of the fundamentals of the company. Cons are that it's not too helpful when evaluating early stage companies and it uses many assumptions like the growth rate and discount rate which could potentially change over time.

Q. What are "comps"?

A. A valuation technique where you create a universe of sample companies by location, capital structure or any other manner in order to find an industry average multiple. The product of that multiple and something like EBTIDA or sales will give us the enterprise value of the target company.

Q. What is precedent transactions analysis?

A. Similar to comps, except here you create a universe of completed deals within the past five years to find an industry average multiple. The product of that multiple and the target company's EBITDA or sales will give us enterprise value.

Q. Which technique will give us the highest valuation?

A. Likely precedent transactions analysis since there is a built-in control premium when a company is purchased.

Q. How do you value a company without cash flows?

A. If the company has assets on hand we can use the asset-backed valuation method, if not we can use the venture capital method to back out a post-money valuation based on the anticipated enterprise value and ROI in the exit year. Once we have post-money valuation we can simply subtract the amount they are asking for to arrive at a pre-money valuation.

Q. Besides the VC method, are there any other ways to value a company pre-revenue?

A. Sure, there are a number of methods developed by angel investors like Bill Payne and Dave Berkus. These are based on the management team and other risk factors. Typically these early stage pre-money valuations are between $2M and $3M.

Q. What does the football field tell us?

A. It gives us a range for each valuation method, allowing us to pinpoint an average valuation for the given company.

Q. If I invested $1M at a 25 percent IRR over a 5-year period what is my return?

A. About 2.5x, so $2.5M.

Q. Let's take that same amount and say we did a little better when we invested it over the next five years at a 30 percent IRR. What is my return?

A. A little more than 4x, so a little more than $10M.

Q. What is the difference between a pre and post-money valuation?

A. The pre-money valuation is the value of a company before we invest while the post-money valuation is the value of a company after we invest.

Q. If a company had a $500k post-money valuation and we invested $250k, how much of the company do we own?

A. We own 50 percent since the post-money valuation implies that the money was already invested.

Q. If a company had a $500k pre-money valuation and we invested $250k, how much of the company do we own?

A. We own ~33.3 percent of the company, since the company is now valued at $750k and we invested $250k.

Chapter 13
# SEMESTER INTERNSHIPS
*HOW TO WORK FOR FREE AND (KIND OF) ENJOY IT*

Many people I spoke with who broke into venture capital out of school had internships during the semester. These internships likely gave them leverage against their fellow students.

While everything discussed in earlier chapters will help you land an opportunity in venture capital, this chapter focuses on what the job entails and how to do it well.

## Adding Value

You will hear this phrase ad nauseam in the venture capital community but it's important. You should have a thorough understanding of what the partners do so you can find a way to add value.

For instance, a large part of the venture capital experience is sourcing companies and creating market maps (google "Tracxn market maps" or "CB Insights" for a detailed example).

If you have a quota of sourcing 20 companies a week. Work hard to source those companies earlier in the week so you can further qualify those leads, which is likely the job of your superior.

Once you qualify the leads you will have a deeper understanding of what the partners and other higher-ups want. This way you are not only showing you truly care about your job, but you are also proving you can be trusted with higher level tasks. You can use a similar strategy with market mapping.

## Feedback on Company

Always have feedback prepared on a particular company the firm is interested in. It is difficult to find a setting to directly express your feedback, but you can often find times to steer a conversation towards others asking for your feedback simply by mentioning the company.

## Asking for People's Time

People will always want to work with you if you are cognizant of how to ask for their time. You beat out a bunch of others for this opportunity, but you still need to campaign for either future recommendations or a full-time offer. Let's dive into the best ways to approach an analyst, associate or partner for a quick chat.

There is always so much to ask during a one-on-one meeting. Venture capital has such a long learning curve, you really don't know if you made a good investment until 5 or more years out. Aside from the learning curve, if they are a partner on the board of a few startups you can talk about what makes a great board member.

If you don't have a relationship with the person you want to chat with, you may want to meet with someone who does first so as to avoid any potentially awkward situations. In general, you can follow a rubric similar to the e-mail-an-entrepreneur/VC e-mail in chapter three. Here is a sample ask you can play around with:

*Hey, I know you're really good at connecting founders with opportunities to grow their companies and being memorable. That's really something I aspire to do as my career moves forward. Would love to learn a little more about how you developed that specific skill set. I know you're slammed, but what does your calendar look like next week for a quick coffee?*

Starting with a compliment or acknowledgment of their skill set shows you are doing your homework and have a genuine inclination to learn more about their craft.

People above you generally want to help you get to their level. After shifting gears into your aspiration to develop a similar skill set, all that's left to do is politely ask for their time.

I usually acknowledge their busy schedule first through something like the above ("I know you're slammed"). Interestingly, I found that if I directly ask for a busy person's time they will say they need to check their calendar. However, if I ask what their calendar looks like over the next week, I was sometimes able to get a meeting on the books in a matter of minutes. Stick with this type of phrasing.

## Asking for More Work

Before asking for more work, make sure the work you already finished is up to par. No one at your firm read that awesome essay about Buddhism you wrote in humanities class. You are being judged here and now on your work product so make it count.

Asking for more work is similar to asking for people's time. You need to be aware of that person's availability, or *bandwidth* at the moment or else you may come off as a nuisance.

You want more work in other areas that will diversify your skill set, but be kind about this; finding the most opportune time is key. You want to get to a point where you have experience in sourcing, market mapping as well as understanding the fundamentals of a great pitch deck. Use the sample below as a reference:

*Hey I learned a lot from sourcing companies in the consumer internet space. I now know why X and Y are so important to Z. I noticed you led the sourcing and mapping efforts in the virtual and augmented reality space. I've always had a strong interest in learning more there. Are there any opportunities to help with sourcing or mapping out that area?*

Always be grateful for the work, but never satisfied. You want to look back on this experience knowing that you have a comprehensive understanding of everything the company does. Showcase a little of what you learned and politely dive into the ask.

## Working Within a Timeline

If your higher-up is asking how soon you can get something done, replying with "How soon do you need this by?" or "How long should this take me?" works fine as well. If you are working on a market map or PowerPoint there is likely a similar project that was completed previously. Always ask if there is a precedent you can look at or use as a reference.

If you are given a timeline—especially if it's your first assignment—and you know you can get something done early, go ahead and finish it early but spend ample time reviewing it. If the work is high quality, you'll be remembered as the person that does great work and hands it in quickly instead of the person that hands things in at the last second. You will benefit from small things like this throughout your internship. As the saying goes: under promise and over deliver.

## Self-Feedback Sessions

In a past summer I worked in investment banking and I was confident I would not get the offer. I thought my dislike for the job was palpable and written all over my face. I was generally quiet for the first half of the internship.

After finishing a few projects with one of the full-time analysts, I asked if he had a few minutes to review my work later in the week.

He took me into one of the conference rooms and let me know that my work product was great, but not a lot of people knew me and it may affect what deals I got staffed on which could affect my offer.

That week I made sure to go out with the team a bit more and the following week I worked on a completely different set of deals, eventually landing an offer to return to the firm.

Feedback sessions like these will help you understand how the firm sees you while showing that you really care about your work product and value input from your colleagues. Don't wait until a mid-summer review to hear feedback, have coffee with one or two colleagues periodically to make sure your work is up to par.

Chapter 14
# EVALUATING A STARTUP
*HOW TO UNDERSTAND ANY MARKET*

## Evaluating Companies

There are many ways to frame the manner in which you should evaluate a company. When I say evaluating, I mean crafting a qualitative understanding of what differentiates one company from another in the same industry.

This question comes up in interviews all the time and this chapter serves as a guideline for you to understand how an investment thesis is implemented. You can also use some of these insights in your company pitch.

One of the most compelling frameworks is proposed by Bill Gurley, an extremely successful early stage investor whose investments include Uber, OpenTable, Zillow and Grubhub.

I will summarize the method here and you can check out his blog for a more detailed approach.[56]

## Doing the Impossible

Ask yourself if the company is creating an entirely new experience, or just making the consumer incrementally better off. Is this a better typewriter or the Apple II? If it is simply a much better typewriter, does it have a "wow" factor that allows the product to surpass rival products?

If you look at a company like OpenTable, consumers previously had about 5 or 6 tabs on their screen and were either searching for reservation details one at a time through each individual site or calling restaurants in order to get an idea of their availability. Now consumers can access over 100 restaurants in the area almost instantly. An entirely new experience indeed.

## Found Money and Found Opportunity

Now think about the economics of a company: is the consumer and supplier better off with this product?

If whoever is supplying the product (either the company or a third party) is receiving *found money*, or in other words an income stream they would otherwise not receive, then the supplier is better off. If the consumer is getting a lower price on the product than they anticipated, the consumer would be better off as well.

With a company like Airbnb, the apartment owner (supplier) is seamlessly receiving found money in a way that would be very difficult without the service. Meanwhile, the short-term renter is likely receiving a much better price than a hotel or else he wouldn't use the service (in economics this is called *revealed preferences*). We can consider Airbnb and other companies creating found money and found opportunity as positively changing the economics of an industry.

## Technology as a Value-Add

Technology can provide data that allows users and firms to work together and create better markets. This can be seen as an extension of positively changing the economics of an industry. Companies like Uber and Upwork provide unprecedented information on their respective industries, enhancing the overall experience of both parties.

## Market Fragmentation

*Market fragmentation* refers to the number of competitors in the space; the more competitors, the more fragmented the market. A highly fragmented market may seem like a negative, but it's actually a great signal that there is no market leader. To venture capitalists, this generally means that no existing company has monetized the industry to the best of its ability and a new entrant has the ability to shake things up in the marketplace.

## TAM (Total Addressable Market)

As discussed earlier, *TAM* is an acronym for total addressable market. TAM represents the market size that the new company will enter, or is currently a player. There are a few caveats with TAM. A company may have the ability to increase the market size upon their success as was the case with OpenTable and restaurant reservations. TAM is a powerful tool when combined with the other evaluation techniques above.

## Network Effect

*Network effects* ask if the experience of customer 200 is better than that of customer 100. In other words, is every customer better off than the one before it?

The idea stems from social networks whose users populate data on a given site, providing the user with more aggregate information in order to make the best decision possible. The principal question to ask is: if the company continues to grow, is the new cohort of consumers better off than the old cohort? Bill Gurley looked at Uber and found that as the company grew, people didn't have to wait as long for a ride. Network effects in action.

## Takeaways

This is not a complete list by any means, but it serves as a guideline for evaluating a startup in any industry. Although this is not a checklist, the more attributes of this framework a company possesses, the more likely they are to become a big player in their respective space.

# Chapter 15
# MOCK CALLS
*HOW TO HANDLE THIS IN AN INTERVIEW*

## Asking the Right Questions

As a VC analyst, you are on the front lines all the time and a large part of the job is sourcing opportunities for the firm. At the interview stage, a partner may ask you to do a mock call in order to get a sense of your ability and intuition when it comes to speaking with companies.

In a mock call you will play the role of the VC and simply ask questions. If the partner chooses to play the role of the entrepreneur, his answers won't necessarily serve as a way to deflect from your overall questions, but instead try to gauge your level of critical thinking and investor lens.

Follow the protocol below if conducting a mock call during an interview.

## Introduce the Firm

> *Hey, great to finally connect. As you know I'm [your name], I work with [firm]. We're a [VC/GE firm] that has a pretty solid track record of [VC firm's message]. [One sentence summary of the firm]. We're also looking for entrepreneurs with great product expertise and a visionary team. We've been looking in the [industry] space and would love to hear a little more about your business.*

Now you can start with the questions.

## Intro Statement and Opening Questions

In a typical meeting with an entrepreneur they will now introduce themselves and their company. It's your responsibility to understand who they are and what they do, but this isn't difficult. The job of the investor is to continually probe into how the business works until we have a clear understanding of their product offering. You can usually disguise this with a hypothetical use case, something like the following:

> So, if I was a [business/consumer] and I needed [present problem], I would use [product offering]?

In an actual meeting, the entrepreneur should provide further clarification and you can feel free to continually probe if necessary. In a mock interview, your interviewer will likely accept your understanding of the business as along as it isn't too far off.

As discussed earlier, companies typical send over a PowerPoint that goes in-depth on the product and financials of the business. Feel free to ask questions regarding the deck in the mock interview after introductions.

> We understand that you're really trying to make this company grow and develop the business. We're impressed with your past performance, but why do you think you'd be able to reach the target numbers you referenced in your pitch?

Here, you are challenging the entrepreneur's understanding of the numbers they are putting forward.

## Anything Changed / What Keeps You up at Night?

> Has anything changed in the use of funds since the business plan?

> What's your perspective on the market or industry, what's keeping you up at night?

You are now digging deeper into any issues or pivots that may have arose in the last few months as well as getting the entrepreneur's take on their sector.

## Larger Scale

*Look, we're really big fans of the product. We wanted to hear your thoughts on any key differentiation points you feel you have. We understand you're sort of the only local player in the area, but on a larger scale, how do you differ?*

As the company scales it needs to be defensible against newer entrants in the market whether that's through the team, IP or a number of other possibilities. Your job here is to find and analyze what makes them defensible and understand whether this will apply to the business at scale.

## Success and a Company's Day-to-Day

*What does success look like to you? What is absolutely critical to your relationship with customers?*

*Who is overseeing the company day-to-day?*

## How to Help

*What do you guys think you need the most help with between now and say, [one year out].*

Here, the entrepreneur will reveal what they need from an investor, which gives you an opening to reiterate your firm's strengths.

## Metrics and Revenue

*How much are you guys burning?*

*What does your churn rate look like?*

*Any insight on your CAC, or how much it costs to acquire a customer?*

*How long is a typical sales cycle?*

*How's (revenue) growth been over the past year?*

Feel free to lay down the above or any other metrics mentioned in the last chapter. Since this is a mock interview your interviewer will reveal these numbers, but there are some scenarios where early stage companies will not reveal specific metrics until VC firms have expressed interest.

If the entrepreneur reveals metrics, ask about their revenue and projected revenue for the next year.

*What does revenue look like for this year? Any idea on projections for next year?*

The core information you want to relay to your firm after a conversation is what the business does, who they sell the product to, any metrics, revenue, growth, projections and your overall thoughts on the business as an investor.

## Exit Opportunities

*What do the exit opportunities look like for a business like this?*

We want to know if the entrepreneur thinks a big strategic company like IBM, Johnson & Johnson or UnitedHealth will purchase the company or if the business is growing so quickly an IPO could be possible in the next few years.

## Anything Else?

*Is there anything else you think we overlooked or anything else you'd like to know about our firm?*

Leave room for the entrepreneur to ask questions or provide any information that they may think is adequate in order for your firm to make an investment decision.

## Takeaways

You are being asked to do the mock interview so the partners know you have a strong sense of how to evaluate a company and an investor lens that can be developed for the next two years. Asking these questions with conviction will give the partners confidence in your ability to find and evaluate deals over the phone and in person on behalf of the firm.

Chapter 16
# START A CLUB
*ALTERNATIVE WAYS TO BREAK IN*

## Entrepreneurship Through Clubs at School

A very admirable way to get on the radar of venture capital firms is to start a program or club whose function is for their members to learn more about venture capital and connect with individuals who work in the industry.

## Columbia Venture Partners

After doing some pro-bono consulting for VC firms and completing a couple VC fellowship opportunities, I really thought I had some valuable information to pass on to anyone that would be interested in a venture capital career.

A few friends and I started what is now known as Columbia Venture Partners, a Columbia University student organization that serves as a training ground for students who are interested in venture capital. We not only train our student-analysts, we also connect them with fellowships and pro-bono consulting opportunities in order to experience what it's like to work in the industry.

Columbia Venture Partners (CVP) is something that's very special to me. I enjoy sharing everything I have learned about venture capital with students who have a genuine passion for the industry and I learn from them every day as well.

The club is fairly new (February 2016), so we recently began the process of partnering with other firms and the results have been incredible. Our analysts have engaged in pitch offs, internships and project-based learning initiatives with firms like Stripes Group, Bowery Capital, Scout Ventures and many more.

## Virginia Venture Fund

I'd be remiss if I didn't mention Virginia Venture Fund (VVF), an organization run by the University of Virginia (UVA) undergraduate student body. I've had many talks with one of their former presidents, Ripley Carroll, regarding strategies and the best practices for starting an analyst program.

Virginia Venture Fund started in 2012 and has been connecting the UVA undergraduate student body with opportunities in venture capital ever since. VVF has a renowned education curriculum which allows students to learn how to evaluate companies from the perspective of a venture capitalist.

The curriculum culminates in a due diligence competition, which has now become an intercollegiate event known as the National Undergraduate Venture Cup.[57]

## Takeaways

Starting a venture capital club or program is a fantastic way to break into the industry. It forces you to lead a team, create and source opportunity where there once was none, and partner with others in your field in order to achieve a greater goal. The examples I mentioned were in an academic setting but can be easily replicated outside of school as well. These are precisely the skills venture capital firms are looking for.

# Chapter 17
# CASE STUDIES
*STORIES FROM OTHERS*

Like many other things, there is more than one way to break into venture capital.

Here are six interviews from individuals who have gained internships and full-time offers. Through these interviews you will learn that the type of person who becomes an investor isn't necessarily someone with a banking or consulting background (although there is plenty of that). There are also those who had previous experience in operational roles at companies or focused there energy on founding a club or startup.

Below they will explain in detail how they broke in and any advice for those aspiring to do the same.

# MADELINE BROOKS

**Babson College '17**
**Incoming Analyst at Stripes Group**

Photo by Craig Warga - www.craigwarga.com

Madeline is currently a senior at Babson College studying finance and entrepreneurship. Below she shares her story of breaking into venture capital and advice for those aspiring to also break in. Madeline is an incoming analyst at Stripes Group, a growth equity firm based in New York City that makes $10-100 million investments in Internet, SaaS, Healthcare IT and Branded Consumer Products.

## How did you know the venture capital industry was right for you?

I've always been an early adopter of technology and I knew I really wanted a job that helped me explore innovation and how different processes work.

I also knew I wanted to get exposure to a lot of different industries so instead of doing a startup and diving into one specific vertical, I wanted a more generalist feel. That's ultimately what led me to VC: the fact that I'd really be able to touch a bunch of different industries and really see innovation throughout all the different ecosystems.

For me it was the best of all worlds because I was able to explore disruptive innovation as well as entrepreneurship in a lot of different industries

### Did you find that you needed to network a lot to get into venture capital?

I definitely think networking is huge for breaking into the industry. My school specifically doesn't have on-campus recruiting in the VC space. For me it was very much an individual process and I think networking provided me with an opportunity to learn about the different industries that you get to touch, different deal stages, firms—talking to people to figure out where you'd fit well in the VC landscape. It was also a way to showcase my passion to people in that community, and the idea that I was serious about getting into the industry.

I think networking as well, it's not just about the people in the VC world but the people who are at startups too, because they have these connections that you really don't think about when you meet them. I think between networking with entrepreneurs, startups and VCs I was always able to show that I was interested in the space. I think that's one of the most important qualifications for breaking in.

### Do you think VCs are looking for more product, business development, finance or entrepreneurial experience? What type of person are they looking for?

Yeah, I don't really think that there's one right area that they focus on or look for in a candidate. More increasingly, it really isn't the finance person, it's more of the engineering person or the arts and sciences person, someone who can bring diversity into the industry.

Banking is great and obviously has its uses in the VC world, but there's so much more to be said for someone who can bring diversity, look at a deal through a different lens and bring in the information that hasn't always circulated in VC firms.

I think at this point in time it's more about what the candidate has done and areas the candidate has touched in a variety of industries, rather than always looking for the finance person or the investment banker. I think it's increasingly more the student who's done the startup and has been able to touch a lot of industries.

### Are there any common mistakes people make when recruiting for venture capital?

I think the biggest mistake is people think there's this checklist of steps they need to complete before being ready for a venture job. Increasingly you'll see this when you talk to students who are graduating college.

They believe that they need either a few years of finance or work experience and then need to go to business school and only after that can they apply for a venture job. That's not necessarily true given the fact that VCs are switching over to a candidate that's more involved with entrepreneurship and startups and definitely has a different background.

I think it's still great to take financial modeling or other courses that will be relevant, but a lot of people think that they need 2-4 years in finance or a 4.0 GPA, but VC is ultimately driven by that passion to find out the companies that are disruptive and find out who the early adopters are.

Forcing passion is something really difficult to do, but usually happens when there is this checklist of things that people believe they need. I think that VC—due to shows like Silicon Valley on HBO—is kind of painted as the ultimate picture of success and a lot of people think they'll be satisfied when they reach VC, which actually also kind of drives the whole checklist thing, but if you don't have passion for combing through all these companies and sourcing and talking to CEOs who are usually a little nervous about taking institutional money, then your success as a VC will be limited.

When people are applying for the position, they need to understand it's a passion-driven job and there's no right way to get into it and no checklist that's necessary to break into the industry.

### What else is important to emphasize on your resume for these types of jobs?

I think it's really important to emphasize any direct impact that you had in your previous job, being your own best advocate and following through with your actions on what you say. For example, if you completed a due diligence task on a SaaS-based recruiting solution for a company you worked for, in your resume make sure you follow up on how that information ultimately impacted the company's success.

Did having the SaaS solution you recommended increase the number of candidates in the pipeline? Did the tool help screen candidates more efficiently which freed up time for recruiters? I think if you provide the impact of your work, you will prove your worth to future employers. I think that's something a lot of people miss and it's an easy way to stand out from the rest of the crowd if you really emphasize your direct impact.

**What would you say to someone who is from a non-core school and wants to pursue this path?**

I think that being your own advocate through the entire process is important. When I went through the process I cold-emailed recruiters and really emphasized my past impact on previous jobs.

If you're able to reach out and succinctly explain why you're best suited for the job and that you'd really just like to meet, I think that's the best first step for a non-core student. Also, looking for experiences that build upon the skills you want to strengthen is great as well, whether that's building upon a sales experience you gained last summer or taking a coding class.

Doing things that strengthen the weaker skills while at the same time being your own best advocate for the skills that you do have is the best way to go.

Also, don't be afraid to contact the firms. Many people believe there's a very rigid recruiting process and they can't call recruiters and can't talk to analysts, but just by reaching out you'll see that people are so generous with their time when it comes to talking with others who show an interest in the industry. I think that just being your own best advocate, reaching out and making the calls and building up your skills will get you to where you want to be and help you break into the industry

**Anything else you'd like to say and how can everyone reach you?**

Yeah sure, feel free to reach out through e-mail at madelinenbrooks@gmail.com. I think the biggest thing is that just because you don't have a checklist, if you're not in finance, if you don't have a 4.0 GPA, if you didn't work in banking or you didn't work at a startup, these aren't things that should hinder your application or potential application into a VC because it's really how you impact the firm as your own person and it's really about you carving your own path, not following in the footsteps of someone else.[58]

# RIPLEY CARROLL

**McIntire School of Commerce, University of Virginia '17**
**Incoming Analyst at Stripes Group**

Ripley is currently a junior in the McIntire School of Commerce at the University of Virginia studying finance and information technology. He is currently the president of the Virginia Venture Fund, a student-led venture capital initiative on campus. Ripley is an incoming summer analyst at Stripes Group, a growth equity firm based in New York City that makes $10-100 million investments in Internet, SaaS, Healthcare IT and Branded Consumer Products.

**Tell me about your background and how you got into venture capital in the first place.**

Sure, I'm a third year at the McIntire School of Commerce majoring in finance and information technology. I was always interested in technology from a young age. I would read things like the MIT Technology Review, Popular Science, a lot of different tech publications of the time.

I started getting into venture capital in my last year of high school. My uncle happened to work for a pretty well known VC firm so I got familiar with the space and it seemed like a really interesting field that mixed technology, business and my interest in entrepreneurship. At UVA I met Matt Brown who founded the Venture Venture Fund (VVF), a student-run VC group here at UVA. I got to do a ton of projects with VC, growth equity and angel firms and my interest in the space matured into what it is today as I moved up the ranks to become president of the organization.

### How did you know the venture capital industry was right for you?

At UVA practically all finance majors go into banking or consulting. It's a relatively new thing for venture capital firms to recruit here, this only happened in the last year or so.

I put myself on the banking track and it really didn't pique my interest. I knew most people didn't necessarily go into venture capital out of undergrad, but I just wanted to start talking to people and see where that led.

I started talking to a few people from VC firms like Columbia Capital, Updata Partners and Anthos Capital. It then dawned on me that these people truly enjoyed their jobs. I realized a large part of their day-to-day activities involved connecting with people on a personal level.

In a lot of finance jobs, you don't get that as much, and that's how I really knew venture capital was right for me. It's a very people-focused business. You have to like people and you have to enjoy networking. For me, I really enjoy that quite a bit.

### Did you have to network a lot to break into VC or did you go through regular on-campus recruiting routes?

There wasn't on-campus recruiting of venture capital here until recently, so essentially it was all networking for me.

I would just say to anyone that's trying to get into this field that networking is extremely important and you have to create your own opportunities.

Some firms have a formal analyst program and that's a straightforward and formal process, but there are a lot of firms that don't have a formal program and could maybe use an analyst. If you call them up and you pitch them, they might want to take you on, but you have to create your own opportunity there.

Also, you can't go from nothing to working in venture capital. You want to either work for a startup first or work in a tangential field and get some experience. I highly recommend working for a startup in business development. I think that's maybe one of the best experiences you can get after your first-year summer.

Another quick tip in general: don't worry about your job description, just think about how you can create value. For most places you may work, especially smaller places, titles don't matter so much. Just impress people with your work product.

### Do you think VCs are looking for more product, business development, finance or entrepreneurial experience? What are your thoughts on that?

If you are sure you want to do banking and you're an excel guy and super into valuation and DCF and everything like that...this is probably not for you. Most of the people I've met in this space are good at those things but they prefer something like a 30/70 split, quantitative to qualitative or they want to understand the story, especially the people behind the numbers at a much deeper level.

They're looking for somebody that can really look into a company and understand how it fits into a larger landscape. Someone who understands trends, actually a great trait you can pick up from consulting as opposed to banking.

I think probably the best background to have: you want a little bit of finance experience, but probably the best background would be some entrepreneurial experience or possibly business development at a startup if you can get it. Maybe you founded your own company or you have some experience at a venture-backed startup.

I worked in business development for a venture-backed startup called Speek. I helped establish partnerships there, made a list of potential acquirers for the company, and participated in conversations with these acquirers throughout the process. Speek ended up getting acquired by Jive Communications, which was one of the companies on my list.

The right mix, I think, is business development, a little bit of finance and a bit of pure sales if you can get that experience.

### Are there any common mistakes people make when recruiting for venture capital?

I think the biggest mistake people make is they think it's a pure finance job and are in it mostly for the money instead of to help entrepreneurs. VC falls under the field of private equity, but it's quite different from LBOs and all that.

Venture capital is a very different path compared to going into banking and then going into an LBO shop. You're going to be doing very different things if you go into venture capital.

A lot of people may come into their first year with a finance job mentality, that's not a good attitude to have for a lot of the firms I have worked with.

Also, if you go to information sessions you really want to try and reach out to people who might not necessarily be trying to talk to you. What I mean is, you want to get access to people who are the real decision makers and who can pull for you personally.

Try and create an opportunity to present yourself in those situations where you can meet the partners of the firm. I've even cold-called firms and asked for informational interviews, there are a lot of people who are afraid to do that type of thing.

Cold calling could really help you get a job at some of the leading growth equity firms. If you cold call them and ask for an interview or an internship, they're going to be really impressed by that. I'd say that's something people should do more of.

**What else is important to emphasize on your resume for these types of jobs?**

I think you need to look at your own experience to make that determination. One thing in general, you do want to emphasize any work you've done for startups or any entrepreneurial experience you have.

I'd actually put that on the top at my resume. In the summer of my sophomore year, I interned at a middle-market firm working with venture debt and I put my business development experience at Speek in my freshman year above my sophomore internship. I thought that pertained more to the work I would do in growth equity, so I think those types of things are important to emphasize.

There are a variety of backgrounds and personalities that could be good at this and you just want to try and show those qualities on your resume. You don't have to order your resume chronologically, order it based on what you think the firm would want to see most.

## Do you recommend starting a venture capital club for students who don't have one currently on their campus?

I actually think that's a really good idea. If you don't have a student venture capital group at your school, go start one. That's the best thing you could possibly do.

VVF gives me a reason to call venture capitalists and it gives them a reason to pick up the phone. When you are the president of a club like this you're not only helping others, but you also have a great opportunity to get in touch with individuals that would otherwise be difficult to reach.

They're going to be interested in hearing more about your organization most likely even if it isn't that large or developed. It's also a platform from which you can hustle, essentially. For instance, VVF has set up a lot of projects with different firms and it gives you a different way to further develop your relationships with some amazing people.

For example, I met for coffee with one of our partners and I brought up the idea of an analyst program. They ended up starting a small analyst class to assist the associates and because I was with VVF I had the opportunity to say, "Hey, there's a bunch of smart guys from UVA here and it'd be great if you did a project with them. I think it'd be a great recruiting tool for you guys to maybe learn more about the students who you might be able to hire. It's the best possible interview experience for you while making the associate's life a little easier."

It just allows me to get to know everyone at the firm much better, to the point where I'm just comfortable sending them an e-mail or calling them up and asking them for advice. It's really taken the relationship to a whole different level and made it likely that if I want to go work at that firm sometime in the future I'll be able to.

The short version of that answer is yes, starting a club like this can be very valuable and I encourage anyone to join one or start one themselves.

## Anything else you'd like to say and how can everyone reach you?

Sure thing. I love hearing from people so if you guys want to just feel free to e-mail me at rbc7aa@virginia.edu.

I would just say that, in my experience, if you really want to go into venture capital…don't let people tell you that you can't do it. Make your own path and just go. Like, just do things. Just start down the path.

Maybe you don't know where you're going to end up or if you'll get there necessarily, but just start doing things that you think will help you. Don't let anyone say you can't do this because the space is "so small" or because "they don't recruit here," you're going to have to get over that.

In my experience, this isn't something a lot of people do. So, you're going to have to be able to go against the current and just have a lot of confidence in yourself. Also, make sure this is something you really want to do. It's not for everyone. It's for a certain type of person and if that's you, you'll know. Don't let people stop you, because it isn't always easy or straightforward.[59]

# NICHOLAS G. ENRIGHT

**Manhattan College '16**
**Founder and President, Manhattan College Venture Group**

Nicholas is a graduate of Manhattan College and the founder and president of Manhattan College Venture Group. Nick has arranged panels at Manhattan College with some of the leading venture capitalists in New York City. He has an authentic interest in venture capital and is creating opportunities in the space for the Manhattan College undergraduate student body. He is currently interviewing for full-time opportunities in venture.

**Tell me about your actual background and how you got into venture capital in the first place.**

Sure, so in high school I always had an interest in starting my own company. I got really interested in the idea of startups, and from there I learned a little more about the New York startup ecosystem. After coming to Manhattan College, I started looking at different internships. I worked at two different startups as a business development intern and as a growth intern. I really liked the environment and culture at both places.

After those experiences, I started to gravitate towards the venture capital space. I liked the idea of working with so many companies and getting a lot of different perspectives. I also have a background as a behavioral research assistant, which fueled my interest in how companies work and what drives people.

**How did you know the venture capital industry was right for you?**

I'm starting to get a good feel for the industry through the Manhattan College Venture Group. As I continue to network with more venture capitalists, the more I find that they're very open-minded people that are willing to help you. It's definitely a very unique industry to work in being that you get the opportunity to work with such a great variety of startups. I think things like this drew me towards the space.

**Let's talk about the club you founded, Manhattan College Venture Group. How did that get started and is this something people can try at other schools?**

I think people can definitely do this at other schools. For me, this whole thing started in the fall of 2015. I had the idea in November and brought it to the faculty advisor of the entrepreneurship club. She really liked the idea and brought it to the faculty advisor of the investment club, we started collaborating from there and working on the idea.

I started looking up different venture capital conferences, I volunteered at a conference up in Boston. I got to see all these pitches, hear feedback and talk to a few VCs one-on-one. They started to give me advice on how I could grow my club and the many ways I could get into venture.

I started going to more events, I went to an event called Brunchwork, which is a startup-meetup hybrid. I met the founder of Brooklyn Bridge Ventures and he gave me some advice on my club and how I could position it in a way that could make it succeed.

I really wanted to grow the entrepreneurship and investment community at Manhattan College because I didn't really feel that there was a strong presence here. I saw this as an opportunity to capitalize on this idea.

I just kept on going to venture capital events. I went to one called Ask-a-VC and met a good majority of the VCs I know now like Justin Wexler and a few others that I'm now fairly close with.

I started thinking about our first event and reached out to one of the associates at ff Venture Capital. We ended up having about 40 people at this event. There were a lot of people interested in the field that didn't necessarily know what venture capital was. The group was really engaged and asked a lot questions. We're getting great responses from the ff Venture Capital guys and that was really big for the club and Manhattan College as a whole.

From there I asked if we could help out with any extra work that their portfolio companies may need and that's pretty much the direction we're headed in now. We're still ironing out a few kinks but we're going to continue with the strategy of working with the portfolio companies of venture firms as well as helping out with investment through research decks, market mapping and things like that.

### It seems like you've done a ton of networking. Do you think that's important to get a job in the industry?

To me, this is one of the top things you can do to get into VC. Especially if you're not from one of the target schools where they recruit. It's important to get your name out there. The venture capital and startup community is tight in New York City. If you get your name out there and show that you're willing to hustle, you'll do really well.

### What type of person do you think VCs are looking for? Do they want someone with product, business development, finance or entrepreneurial experience?

I think they definitely like people with financial experience or people that have started their own company or have held important roles at a venture-backed startup. If you can show that you can communicate on a high level, you can set yourself apart from others. I think it's also important to just be an amicable person since you're working with a small group of people for such a long period of time.

### What else is important to emphasize on your resume for these types of jobs?

Well I'd say that if you're not at one of the target schools that VCs recruit from then you need to find a way to differentiate yourself greatly. You need something that's going to put you ahead of the pack and separate you. I think that's what I've tried to do with my club. If you've ever started a company, club or had experience at a startup I'd emphasize that at the top.

Aside from the resume, another way to be impactful is to show or prove that you can do the work of a VC. Try and help out with suggestions for their portfolio companies. If you know about a company and think it may be worth a VC's time, always feel free to reach out. I think some of these things are more important than a resume in some aspects. In my experience, the actual interactions I've had with VCs are more valuable than what was actually on my resume.

**What is your advice for some of the readers that are from a non-target school? Would you advise starting a student VC club?**

Yes, I would say starting a club would help. Starting Manhattan College Venture Group was an idea that I worked on for a few months with faculty and advisors. I'd suggest that if you want to get started quickly you may want to start something like this as a branch of a bigger club, like an entrepreneurship club or a branch of the investment club. It's definitely a good way to separate yourself from the pack.

**Anything else you'd like to say and how can everyone reach you?**

Just reach out to me via e-mail: nenright29@gmail.com. Definitely just keep at it. It's probably one of the hardest industries to get into.

Don't get discouraged from some of the things people might say. And you know what, if you don't get in you should go and start your own company.

Find something similar that you're really passionate about. Something that consumes your mind from the day-to-day. You'll be getting great experience that a VC would look for in terms of recruiting.[60]

# JUSTIN WEXLER

**Olin Business School, Washington University in St. Louis '15**
**Associate at WndrCo**
**Former Analyst at Technology Crossover Ventures**

Justin is currently an Associate at a new firm called WndrCo after two years as an Investment Analyst at Technology Crossover Ventures, a leading growth equity firm with investments in Netflix, Spotify, and Facebook. He graduated from the Olin Business School at WashU in 2015 with a degree in finance and marketing. During his time at WashU he interned with Landmark Ventures as a summer associate and Zimmerman Advertising as a strategy intern. He is extremely active in the New York venture space and currently serves as the VC-in-residence for Columbia Venture Partners.

**Tell me about your background and how you gained an interest in venture capital.**

I guess I had a pretty unique background, I grew up in Florida. Not a lot of venture firms out there so I didn't know too much about this going in. I decided to go into the business school at WashU to study business before going to law school. When I realized that a lot of students were leveraging their business skill set to find jobs and not necessarily go right to grad school, I started getting really curious about what was out there.

I did an internship in New York City at a firm called Landmark Ventures and a lot of what they do there is consult with software businesses and that was my first experience with the tech community here in the city.

I really liked the fact that it's very collaborative unlike law, which in many ways forces you to go against everybody else in the trial. So, I really like that aspect of the technology world where you get to help other people build businesses and often times connect others to potential customers or grow businesses; it's a really positive and innovative community.

## How did you know the venture capital industry was right for you?

I get to be in a role that drives business for venture capital and I get to try and find great companies every day and hopefully execute on investing in them.

I love that I get to meet a lot of different people, which was really interesting especially right out of college. Every day I meet with new companies, new executives from those companies, other VC firms, sometimes even bankers if they have clients we'd be willing to invest in. I'm always constantly meeting new people in a lot of industries like manufacturing, construction, security, travel and hospitality.

TCV invests in a lot of areas and I got to talk to the experts that have gone out and created successful businesses, form relationships with them and provide value because I represented a firm that could provide not just capital but expertise in continued growth.

## Did you have to network at all to get your position?

Yup, you have to network a ton. For me I pretty much reached out to every VC in the country.

I really liked my experience in NY and wanted to be here but I also reached out to firms in Boston, Chicago, SF, Los Angeles, DC and even San Diego. I was surprised actually that people responded and actually wanted to talk to me and spend their time with me to share their experiences.

It's good to remember that you have an easier time doing this as a student than as a graduate or person in the workforce because then you can always go under the pretense that you're learning and interested in the space. You'll never know if someone is willing to talk or not unless you reach out.

**Do you think venture capitalists are looking for any particular type of person? For instance, someone with product, business development, finance or entrepreneurial experience?**

All those skills are really important. But in a lot of ways you are marketing your firm and you need the ability to form relationships with people. Often times, I'm introducing CEOs to my firm and you have to be able to tell your firm's story to people.

So yeah, there's a marketing aspect, there's a financial aspect, there's understanding technology and that aspect of it as well. Also, understanding the broader economy is necessary because we invest in technology companies that disrupt other industries whether it's travel, hospitality or any of the other ones I mentioned.

You have to be able to understand the trends in those industries as well. There's just so much to learn and even the partners are learning so much every day. You don't really have to have all of these skills fully developed. As a student, I didn't have all of these skills and still don't in a sense, but you have to at least have the willingness to try and meet people and be pretty assertive. I'm trying not to use the word "hustle" here, but you really have to stand out among all the other candidates and go after it because it's not just going to come to you.

**Are there any common mistakes people make when recruiting for venture capital?**

I would say relying on career fairs or job postings isn't necessarily that helpful. I didn't get any of my internships or jobs based off of those postings. It was all about reaching out to a person.

I mean, even if you do see a good opportunity on a job posting, I would try and see who posted it or if you can't find that, find who would be the person to talk to and just reach out to them directly either through e-mail, phone or LinkedIn.

You could think of a job posting as an official route of getting this job, but at the end of the day it's just people reading your submission and most likely they're just hiring people who they know or who they've connected with in some way or another. Try and be that person instead of the person who only submits online. A big mistake is just filling out forms instead of reaching out to people.

**When it comes to your resume, what do you think is important to emphasize?**

I think it's important to show that you were a leader in some sense or another. Not always like a president of a club or a founder of a club or company, but it's always great to make an impact in some way whether it's through a club or something off-campus. That's the biggest thing. Also, if I see an experience where you have to present in front of other people, that's a big thing to me because it's a huge part of my job.

**What would you say to someone with more of an engineering or computer science background? How should they approach breaking into venture capital?**

I would say the same thing. Even with all the knowledge that comes with hard sciences, you're going to spend a ton of time talking with people. If you're uncomfortable with that I'd advise working on those softer skills because that's a big part of the job. This is the type of job where you start conversations with strangers every day.

**Anything else you'd like to say and how can everyone reach you?**

Reach out to me on Twitter: @JustinAWexler.

You have to be able to tell your story, that's how I got this job. A big reason I've been able to get jobs in VC is because I can tell my story well. I could tell them how I went from my marketing internship, to taking on a finance major and finance internship, to talking about my interest in technology and really being able to speak to all of that in a concise and coherent way.

Also, I was prepared. I learned all I could online about the firm and I do that with all my interviews. I came in with a 36-page book of companies and each page had interesting businesses that I thought would be good investments for the firm.

All that information was free and available on the Internet, but I was the guy who put it together and presented it to the partner I was speaking to. My advice is to just make the most of the opportunity and show how you can be valuable instead of just hoping that they trust what you're saying and take your word for it.[61]

# BRANDON GREER

**Cornell University '16**
**Analyst at OpenView Venture Partners**

Brandon is currently an investment analyst at OpenView Venture Partners. He graduated from Cornell University in 2016 with a degree in Applied Economics and Management. During his time at Cornell, before coming to OpenView, Brandon worked as an investment banking summer analyst at J.P. Morgan.

**Tell me about your background and how you got an interest in venture capital.**

I suppose I knew VC was right for me since I was a kid, although I thought of it in much simpler terms. Ultimately, venture capital is driven by the same quid pro quo framework that enabled my middle school smoothie and snow cone stand: one can acquire capital for their venture in exchange for some ownership. And, with the capital can come an actual partnership, one that benefits the founder beyond mere funding, as well as an opportunity to build something great. My parents were my first venture partners—and will always be somewhat symbolically—and empowered me to think like an entrepreneur. Their term sheet was far less dilutive than any tech founder should expect: I got money for a blender, snow shaver, and a table while maintaining 100 percent ownership. Great deal.

On a more serious note, I knew VC was right for me because I was itching to be more creative and to be myself in just about every professional environment I was part of. In VC, "different" and "unfamiliar" are fundamentally necessary, which of course means that creativity is necessary. This stuck out to me. And, while I'm no guru, I've found confirmation of this in my work, just several months in. I feel challenged to be innovative in my thinking. That alone is freeing.

**Did you have to network a lot to get into VC or did you go through the regular on-campus recruiting routes?**

The short answer is yes. My breaking into VC out of college was definitely the result of networking; but, I mean networking in a much less rigid sense. Much like venture capitalists have to replace cold calls with "warm intros"—that is, founders are far more inclined to speak to investors that they believe to be truly interested in the product or venture—it is likewise tough to begin a conversation with a VC firm in a way that is purely rooted in self-interest or getting a job. So, it's not much of a surprise that I started my interview process with OpenView from a referral.

Like many, I'm lucky to have mentors—some well beyond retirement and others my own age. There's something to learn from anyone. Arsham Memarzadeh, an associate at OpenView, is one of them. He got me connected to the firm and each interview that followed after that introduction reaffirmed my interest in joining. Arsham and I knew one another from college at Cornell, but I was confident he knew of me as more of a person and less as a candidate. VC firms are generally much smaller than your typical out of college top firms, so it's important to know the people you're working with. Plus, interviews should never be a one-way street.

**Do you think venture capitalists are looking for any particular type of person? For instance, someone with product, business development, finance or entrepreneurial experience?**

I can only really speak to OpenView, but every junior VC on the team has a vastly different background, which I predict is by design. We all think differently and that's why it's best to be yourself when you are recruiting in VC, because your personality may balance another and your skillset may compensate where there is a missing link.

## Are there any common mistakes people make when recruiting for venture capital?

Of course! You'll notice a theme in my interview, but in many cases, these mistakes stem from people not being themselves. No person out of college can be expected to know the full industry landscape of vertical software or that of machine learning-enabled chat bots. Perhaps you are an expert, but if you're not, it's ok to convey interest over expertise.[62]

# JASON SHEIN

**University of Pennsylvania '17**
**Incoming Analyst at General Atlantic**

Jason is currently a senior at the University of Pennsylvania in the Science, Technology and Society (STSC) program. He briefly studied organizational psychology at the Stockholm School of Economics in Sweden and has interned for Compound Ventures as well as the Brooklyn Nets. I interviewed Jason after he was offered a summer analyst role at General Atlantic, a leading global growth equity firm that makes $25-400 million investments in emerging retail and consumer markets, Internet and Technology, financial services and healthcare. After graduating, Jason will return to General Atlantic as an analyst in the Internet and Technology group focusing on emerging growth opportunities.

**Tell me about your background and how you got an interest in venture capital.**

I played sports all throughout high school and became really interested in nutrition, fitness, healthy living and how these things intersect with technology.

I took computer science in high school, came to UPenn and found the STSC major (Science, Technology and Society). I started studying the history of science and tech while doing a minor in Engineering Entrepreneurship.

I got into some investment clubs on campus and really became interested in VC through my experiences there. I ended up landing a gig at Compound Ventures, an early stage firm in New York City and then went through the process of figuring out whether I wanted to work at a startup or go the investing route and see how a diverse set of companies develop in growth equity and late stage VC. So, I chose the VC route.

**How did you know this industry was right for you?**

I think I was really excited about the flat nature of VC. I worked at a huge corporate company in the past and didn't really like that big anonymous company culture, so I checked that off my list of what I didn't want to do.

I didn't have a deep knowledge of the tech verticals and landscapes, so I thought meeting with great companies and entrepreneurs and seeing their cutting-edge technologies would definitely be the right way to start out.

**For your sophomore internship at Compound Ventures, what were some of the things that made you stand out in the interview?**

I think the interview process was pretty informal. At smaller firms, it's much more difficult to develop an analyst program or an interview process for a program so it came down to a lot of calls or hopping by the office when I was in New York. I think it was really about maintaining that point of contact and relationship.

Every so often I would send an e-mail with a new startup or ping the guys at Metamorphic about some news in their space. I talked about the startups I was interested in, but I think at the end of the day it came down to a culture fit.

**Did you rely on campus recruiting or did you have to network a lot to break into venture capital?**

It was definitely 100 percent networking. You have to leverage every connection here and there and really put yourself out there.

I got in touch with the Compund guys in October and only got the offer in March. While I ended up meeting them through a personal connection, it still took a while to foster that connection into a summer offer.

I constantly scraped through LinkedIn and set up phone calls with friends and alumni to try and figure out the best way to move forward. It's kind of like you need to throw a bunch of stuff at the wall and hope that a few things stick, I think that really worked out.

**Do you think VCs are looking for any specific type of person? Do you think they like more finance, product, business development or entrepreneurial experience?**

Well I think there are a few different ways to approach that question. First, the stage is really important. If we're looking early stage, finance is not necessarily a relevant background.

Having more technical experience at an early stage is definitely more advantageous although less necessary because what you're likely doing is staying up to date on what's new and relevant in a given space.

I think the folks at Metamorphic were looking for somewhat of a self-starter or hustler who was really excited about technology, could learn on their own and constantly come up with new ways to find companies.

I think it was important that I had a thirst for technology. It was something I already spent most of my time doing.

**Are there any mistakes you think people make when recruiting for venture capital jobs?**

You know, I think that sometimes people may focus too much on being formal, which I think is a common mistake when you're coming from some of these private schools where a lot of kids are looking to go into finance.

Also, if you want to differentiate yourself you can show that in other ways besides your resume. Send a pitch deck or a project you've done or anything of that nature. I think there are a lot of talented people out there that don't know how to sell themselves as well as they could.

**What's important to emphasize on your resume?**

I guess if you don't have a lot on your resume it's really important to discuss a vertical that you're interested in.

If you only did one project in a certain space it's important to say, "Hey, I may only have this one experience but I learned x, y and z from that. I could add value by breaking down companies in this sector perhaps better than the other candidates."

**What would you say to someone with more of an engineering or computer science background? How should they approach breaking into venture capital?**

Well I do think VC is going more into that direction, looking more at technical people and product people.

They almost don't even need to sell themselves as much on those technical skills as much as just showing their background, and what they've worked on in the past. Show that you're able to understand markets and read up on competitive landscapes.

Try to avoid painting yourself as someone who just sits at a computer and lacks some of the business development skills that make VCs successful.

**Can you touch on your interview experience at General Atlantic? How did you prepare for that?**

Well I think that what they really want to see is a thirst and passion for technology, that's perhaps the most important. Second, is someone who is really excited about different verticals and able to discuss companies within a given industry.

You don't need to have the right answers, necessarily; it's the thought process that matters most. It's about saying you're excited about digital health because of x, y or z trend and then speaking about companies that operate within that trend. Then going into why you would choose this company versus their competitors or incumbents.

Having that type of knowledge, thought process and logic was really important and I really prepared there. Lastly, you have to be able to sell yourself from a fit and personal standpoint. I think the way you do that really takes some self-reflection and practice, but at the end of the day—some of the best advice I got actually—was to make the goal of the interview a conversation.

So not one person screening another, but really just a friendly casual conversation describing who you are and really who you want to be at the firm and doing what that position offers.

Be prepared to just talk about yourself. Practice a bunch and have friends ask you random questions during mock interviews. That will help you be ready for the questions that you may not be able to predict.

**Anything else you'd like to say and how can everyone reach you?**

In terms of contacting me, feel free to reach me through my e-mail: jshein@sas.upenn.edu.

One last thing I'll say, for people that are trying to get into VC, the best way to do it is to leverage those connections and reach out to as many people as possible.

Even if a phone call or conversation may not seem that helpful to you, if you have the opportunity in some way, shape or form I'd say take it. Once you throw all those things at the wall that's how things stick. If a particular connection doesn't pan out for you right away, it doesn't mean it can't in the next 6 months or so down the line.

The other thing I'll add to that is the importance of differentiating yourself. Try not to just send a resume and cover letter. Send a project that you worked on, or put together a video cover letter of yourself. Do something creative that matches your skills and makes someone want to take the call or read the e-mail instead of just moving on with their day.[63]

# Chapter 18
# CONCLUSION

As you continue to break into this industry, I hope you stay in touch with me and this book serves you well. Sign up for my mailing list at breakintovc.com for your free white paper on how to pitch a company and my latest blog posts. Feel free to reach out to me at bradley@breakintovc.com or any of the interviewees at any time in the future.

The idea here is to create a community of venture capital enthusiasts who can continually learn from each other and grow, regardless of where we all end up.

Here is a list of early and late stage venture capital firms that have made an effort to recruit at one time or another. Some have established programs, and others you will need to look at more closely to find an opening.

If a firm only has 1 or 2 analysts or associates, it's likely that individual will only stay at the firm for two years before moving on. Reach out at the 1.5 year mark, and try to market yourself to land an interview on cycle.

Stripes Group (New York, NY)

Insight Venture Partners (New York, NY)

Technology Crossover Ventures (Palo Alto, CA and New York, NY)

General Atlantic (New York, NY)

JMI Equity (Baltimore, MD)

Bessemer Venture Partners (New York, NY)

Union Square Ventures (New York, NY)

Bain Capital Ventures (Boston, MA and New York, NY)

KEC Ventures (New York, NY)

Level Equity (New York, NY)

Scout Ventures (New York, NY)

Spectrum Equity (Boston, MA)

Thrive Capital (New York, NY)

Susquehanna Growth Equity (Bala Cynwyd, PA)

North Bridge Growth Equity and Venture Partners (Waltham, MA)

NextGen Venture Partners (Washington, D.C.)

Spring Lake Equity Partners (Boston, MA)

Trident Capital (Palo Alto, CA)

Updata Partners (Washington, D.C.)

Volition Capital (Boston, MA)

Lead Edge Capital (New York, NY)

Anthos Capital (Los Angeles, CA)

Access Partners (San Francisco, CA)

Kleiner Perkins Caufield & Byers (San Francisco, CA)

GSV Acceleration (Chicago, IL)

OpenView Venture Partners (Boston, MA)

Battery Ventures (Boston, MA)

March Capital Partners (Los Angeles, CA)

Vocap Partners (Atlanta, GA)

Ringleader Ventures (Chicago, IL)

Sierra Ventures (San Francisco, CA)

Alsop Louie Partners (San Francisco, CA)

Armory Square Ventures (New York, NY and Syracuse, NY)

FF Venture Capital (New York, NY)

Bullpen Capital (San Francisco, CA)

General Catalyst (Palo Alto, CA)

Vista Equity Partners (San Francisco, CA)

Altamont Capital Partners (Palo Alto, CA)

Pear VC (Palo Alto, CA)

Venrock (Palo Alto, CA)

# GLOSSARY

*Accelerator*

Works with a company at the earliest stages of their lifecycle usually on a fixed-term basis. The programs include mentorship and often education elements, ultimately culminating in a presentation or pitch to investors and seasoned entrepreneurs.

*Accounts Payable*

Companies usually purchase goods and services on credit. Between the time they receive the good or service and the time they actually pay, the amount owed will be listed on their books as a liability under accounts payable on the balance sheet.

*Accounts Receivable*

Short-term money that a company is owed or will collect within one year. Between the time they sell the good or service and the time the receive cash, the incoming amount will be listed as an asset under accounts receivable on the balance sheet.

*Additional Paid-In Capital*

The price paid by the investor over the par value. If we wanted to raise $20M and the common stock value is $100,000, the remaining portion is put in additional paid-in capital. This comes out to $19.9M.

*Alternative Investments*

An asset that is not a traditional investment, such as a stock or bond. Alternative investments are usually held by large organizations like pension funds and life insurance companies. Examples include private equity (venture capital) and real estate.

*Annualized Run Rate (ARR)*

An accurate depiction of company's forecasted revenue for the year. Generally speaking, take the amount of revenue that is recurring within the given month and multiply by 12.

*Asset-Based Valuation*

Used when a company has no cash flow, is near bankruptcy and preparing to liquidate assets for sale. Asset-based valuation also comes in handy when a company's value can be largely derived from its tangible and intangible assets. At a high level, take the value of all assets and subtract the value of all liabilities.

*Assets*

What a company owns. Assets represent all sorts of items like machinery, land, factories, inventory, cash, accounts receivable and anything else that can be expressed in dollars. Assets are represented on the balance sheet and are bought to increase the value of firm.

*Balance Sheet*

The balance sheet is a snapshot in time of what a company owns and owes, in other words their financial position. Like the other financial statements, the balance sheet of a company can be seen on quarterly reports and annual reports. The three sections of the balance sheet are assets, liabilities and shareholders' equity. Assets must equal or balance with liabilities and shareholders' equity.

*Bandwidth*

A person's availability in a given time frame.

*Berkus Method*

Named after Dave Berkus, an early stage valuation technique for pre-revenue businesses. The method has a pre-money valuation cap of $2.5M.

*Black-Scholes Model*

A theoretical model formulated in 1973 to value a company as an option.

*Book Value (of a Company)*

The reported assets of a company less its intangible assets (like patents) and liabilities.

*Book-to-Bill Ratio*

A metric to make predictions on the cash flow and financial health of a business. When a company books an order, they are receiving a request for the product or service. When a company bills an order, they have a request for the good or service to be fulfilled. A book-to-bill ratio of less than one shows weak demand while a ratio greater than one shows strong demand.

*Bookings*

When a customer signs up for a service but the company has not delivered that service yet. Bookings could be as elementary as a customer signing up on a website or more contractual in nature.

*Burn Rate*

The amount of venture capital cash used or "burned" in a given period by a startup, usually a monthly metric.

*CAC Payback Period*

How long it takes to recover the cost of acquiring a customer. The ideal time for startups to recoup this cost is 12 months or less.

*Capitalization Table*

An account of all shareholders in a private company broken down into their percentage of ownership and value of equity in each fundraising round.

*Carried Interest*

The share of the profits that partners receive after the amount invested has been returned. In venture capital, this is commonly 20 percent of future profits.

*Cash*

Currency or its equivalent that can be accessed immediately or in the near short-term.

*Cash Flow from Financing*

The flow of cash between the company and its creditors. Anything that has to do with raising money or repaying shareholders will fall into CFF.

*Cash Flow from Investing*

The flow of cash from the buying and selling of long-term assets like buildings and heavy machinery.

*Cash Flow from Operations*

The flow of cash from ongoing core business activities like sales of goods or services.

*Cash Flow Statement*

Allows a business to see the cash inflows and outflows in a given period.

*Changes in Working Capital*

Since working capital is current assets minus current liabilities, changes in working capital measures this difference across the periods.

## Chicago Method

A discounted cash flow (DCF) method using three scenarios (success, sideways and failure), estimating the probability of each in order to get a more realistic enterprise value of a company.

## Churn Rate / Logo Churn

Churn rate usually refers to the attrition rate of customers—or number of customers lost—in a given period, but it can be used in a number of other instances (employees, board members, dollars retained and other scenarios). The term is usually synonymous with logo churn, which specifically refers to the loss of customers in a given period.

## Cost of Goods Sold (COGS)

Also referred to as cost of sales, COGS are any expenses incurred for producing a good or service. This includes raw materials, labor or any manufacturing costs required to make all products sold.

## Collections

As opposed to bookings, collections are recorded when money is actually collected from the customer. This can occur before or after services are rendered.

## Committed Capital

Cash received or requested by a general partner of a venture firm from a limited partner. Partners request the committed capital whenever the firm decides to invest.

## Common Stock

Shares that represent a certain percentage ownership of a company. To calculate common stock value of a company, multiply the par value by the number of shares issued.

## Comparable Companies Analysis ("Comps")

A method of valuing a company by creating a universe of several sample companies that all have one thing in common (location, product, industry, geography, debt structure etc.).

## Contra-Equity Account

An equity account where cash is flowing out of the business. Treasury stock is considered a contra-equity account.

*Control Premium*

The cost a business will pay for an acquisition above what the company is worth on paper or what the market deems to be accurate.

*Current Assets*

Assets like cash, accounts receivable and inventory that can indeed be consumed or liquidated in one year.

*Current Liabilities*

These are obligations that are due or owed within a given period. Common examples are accounts, salaries and interest payable.

*CLV/CAC Ratio*

Ratio that tells us for every dollar a company spends on acquiring a new customer, the company will generate "x" in value over the lifetime of that customer.

*Customer Acquisition Cost (CAC)*

The cost of acquiring a new customer. Costs typically tucked into CAC are advertising, PR, base pay for sales people as well as commission, sales manager salaries, any on-boarding costs and any other business or industry-specific costs. The lower your CAC the better.

*Customer Lifetime Value (CLV)*

The projected revenue that a customer will bring for a company during their lifetime as a customer. Since customer acquisition and marketing can be expensive, metrics like CLV help determine just how much to spend to acquire a customer beforehand. If a company is spending more than CLV to acquire a customer, they may actually lose money in the long run.

*Debt*

The amount of money a company owes. Debt can be used to purchase a service or entire businesses a company may not be able to afford with just cash as is the case with private equity firms. Debt can also be used as a way for startups to receive cash without giving up equity. Debt holders get paid out first before equity holders.

*Debt Financing*

Taking out a loan in order to purchase an asset, in the case of private equity funds, usually the majority of a business.

*Debt Covenants*

Requirements or restrictions that a company may need to meet or follow (performance metrics, raising more debt etc.) in order to get the full amount of financing over time from a venture firm.

*Deferred Revenue*

Revenue that has yet to be accounted for and is therefore a liability for a company. An example may be revenue received for a sporting event before that event has taken place.

*Depreciation and Amortization (D&A)*

A measurement of the cost or decay of a physical asset over its lifetime. If it is a physical asset the method is referred to as depreciation, otherwise with line items like patents or media licensing, the method is referred to as amortization.

*Dilution*

Usually referring to a reduction in ownership or value between financing rounds.

*Discount Rate*

The rate at which company discounts the "future dollars" of a target company in order to arrive at the present value.

*Discounted Cash Flow (DCF)*

A valuation technique where a business takes all the money that a target company is estimated to make in the foreseeable future (usually five years), and converts those "future dollars" to "present day" dollars.

*Dividends*

Payments made to shareholders. A company may issue dividends in cash or additional shares.

*Dividend Recapitalization ("Dividend Recap")*

Dividends paid to the private equity firm and other shareholders on behalf of the portfolio company.

*Dollar Revenue Retention (DRR)*

The amount of revenue you are retaining from your customers or a cohort in a given period. The metric is largely used in the Software-as-a-Service (SaaS) industry and others that have tiered pricing.

*Downside Protection*

Limiting or reducing the losses on a portfolio or investments through covenants or a more constrained investment thesis.

*EBITDA*

Earnings before interest, tax, depreciation and amortization. Since many companies have different tax rates and ways to account for interest, EBITDA is a line item that investors can use to compare one company to another.

*Enterprise Value*

The value of the entire firm. All valuation techniques are trying to arrive at an accurate enterprise value. This is how much a business should pay for a target company.

*Equity*

An equity stake refers to the percentage ownership of a target company the venture firm will receive after investment. Equity holders are paid out after debt holders.

*Equity Financing*

When a company sells some number of private stock shares to a venture firm who pays in cash or its equivalent.

*Equity Value / Market Capitalization*

In the context of enterprise value, equity value is the total value of a company's stock, otherwise known as the market capitalization of a company.

*Football Field*

A singular graph detailing the range of each valuation method in order to arrive at a proper final value that intersects all or most of the valuation techniques used.

*Found Money*

The concept of a business allowing a supplier to receive an income stream that they otherwise would not have received (Airbnb hosts, Uber drivers etc.).

*Free Cash Flow (FCF)*

Money that is left over after core expenses like paying employees, advertising and keeping the lights on. Free cash flow is the money that is forecasted into the future when valuing a target company.

*Generally Accepted Accounting Principle (GAAP)*

Accounting standards set by the Securities and Exchange Commission (SEC) that a company must follow in their financial statements. Consistency allows for investors and general public to more easily analyze financial data.

*Gross Profit / Gross Margin*

The result of subtracting cost of goods sold (COGS) from net revenue, allowing the business to see the amount left over to pay other expenses. Gross margin is the profitability ratio that shows the amount of gross profit the business will receive for every dollar in net revenue.

*Gross Transaction Value (GTV)*

The total value of all transactions regardless of where the revenue flows. An e-commerce business may only receive 15 percent of all transactions (net revenue), but GTV accounts for this in addition to the other 85 percent.

*Growth Equity*

Minority investments in late-stage companies (Series C, D, E, etc.) in order to have the company either IPO or get acquired. Growth equity investments are typically businesses that are leaders or emerging leaders in their industry, have a few million in revenue, high gross margins and are on their way to becoming profitable businesses.

*Harvest Year*

The year a venture firm will exit a business, commonly referred to as the exit year.

*Headwinds*

A nautical term referring to the concerns or caveats that a company may face in the future. Address headwinds in your analysis of any company.

*Income Statement*

Also referred to as the profit and loss (P&L) statement, the income statement allows investors to understand the financial performance and profitability of a company in a given period.

*Income Tax*

The portion of earnings that companies pay towards the government. US corporate income tax is about 39 percent.

*Initial Public Offering (IPO)*

When a private company issues stock to the general public on an exchange and becomes a public business entity. This is the first time a private company issues stock to the public.

*Interest Payable*

A company may owe interest, but not pay upfront. Interest payable represents their obligation to pay interest that is owed within the period.

*Internal Rate of Return (IRR)*

An annualized growth rate that accounts for cash inflows and outflows within the period. IRRs are a performance metric to evaluate investment portfolios usually over a 5 to 10 year time horizon.

*Leveraged Buyout (LBO)*

An acquisition tactic where private equity firms take out sizable loans to buy a company while only investing 30 or 40 percent of their cash. Firms use the high cash flow of the target company to repay the debt.

*Liability*

Represents what a company owes. Typical liabilities are accounts, salaries and interest payable. Liabilities can be found on the balance sheet of a business.

*Limited Partners*

The endowments, foundations, public pensions and high net worth individuals that fund venture capital firms.

*Line of Credit*

An arrangement between a creditor and a company that establishes a maximum loan balance the company can draw from in a given period of time.

*Long-Term Asset*

An asset that is not fully consumed in one year, like a factory or heavy machinery.

*Tailwinds*

A nautical term that represents the positive trends or benefits the company will experience in the near future. An example may be the favorable regulatory landscape where a company wishes to expand.

*Market Fragmentation*

Referring to the structure of the market in terms of the number of competitors in the space. The more competitors, the more fragmented the market. A highly fragmented market may seem like a negative, but is actually a great signal that there is no market leader and successful new entrants may have the potential to gain market share.

*Mergers & Acquisitions (M&A)*

When a business uses any means of debt or equity to purchase a target company, or come to terms in order to unite the two companies into one new business.

*Minimum Viable Product (MVP)*

An early stage in a company's lifecycle where they begin to develop a lean prototype of their product or service offering.

*Minority Interest*

When a business purchases a majority share in a target company, minority interest represents the equity of the subsidiary company that the parent company does not own.

*Minority Stake*

Purchasing less than 50 percent of a company. This is an overarching investment principle of the venture capital asset class.

*Monthly Recurring Revenue (MRR)*

All revenue in a month that is contractually obligated to recur next month.

*Net Income*

The bottom line of the income statement. What a business has earned in a given period after all expenses and taxes in a given period.

*Net Interest Expense*

The cost a company pays for borrowing funds. This is a nonoperating expense that indicates the interest on all types of debt or lines of credit.

*Net Present Value (NPV)*

The present value of a company after accounting for all cash inflows and outflows. The internal rate of return metric is the rate at which the NPV of all the company's cash flows are equal to zero.

*Net Revenue*

The revenue a company will take in after accounting for all gross transactions. If a marketplace business like Upwork receives 15 percent of a $100 transaction in a given period, net revenue is $15.

*Network Effect*

When the experience of customer 200 is better than that of customer 100. The idea stems from social networks whose users populate data on a given site, providing the user with more aggregate information in order to make the best decision possible. This gives every subsequent customer more information than the previous customer.

*Non-Current Liabilities*

Also known as long-term liabilities these are obligations that are not payable within a year and are usually summed up as long-term debt.

*Non-Operating Expense*

Expenses outside of production (COGS and OPEX) like depreciation and amortization as well as net interest expense.

*Operating Expenses (OPEX)*

A set of production expenses encompassing several different cost buckets, namely sales, general and administrative expenses (SG&A) as well as research and development (R&D).

*Operating Profit / Operating Margin*

A GAAP financial measure of the profit earned from a company's core business activities. Operating profit is typically calculated as revenue less COGS less OPEX less D&A. Operating margin is the profitability ratio that indicates the amount of operating profit a company earns for every dollar in net revenue.

*Paid-In Capital (PIC)*

The amount of capital investors have "paid-in" to a business. Otherwise known as the amount of money a company has raised.

*Par Value*

The minimum floor value of a stock. No shares may be sold at a price below this amount.

*Post-Money Valuation*

The value of a company immediately after the latest amount of venture capital is invested.

*Pre-Money Valuation*

The value of a company before that latest round of capital has been invested. Most valuation methods are an attempt to find the pre-money valuation.

*Pre-Tax Income (EBT)*

The earnings of a business before corporate income taxes. After accounting for taxes the next line-item in general net income.

*Precedent Transactions Analysis*

A valuation technique focused on similar (industry, geography, debt structure etc.) transactions that occurred usually in the past five years.

*Preferred Stock*

A share of a company's stock that holds no voting rights but gives fixed, or recurring dividends. Preferred shareholders are paid out before common stock shareholders but after debt holders.

*Present Value*

The value of a company after discounting all future cash flows. The higher the discount rate, the lower the present value.

*Primary Shares*

New shares of stock that are issued from the company and sold to investors.

*Pro-Rata*

Follow-on investment or participation in future rounds of fundraising to maintain the same stake in ownership. An early stage firm may not want to invest pro-rata in late stage rounds not only because it goes against their investment thesis, but also would be difficult to maintain a higher ROI on the fund.

*Property, Plant and Equipment (PP&E)*

Long term assets that are purchased and account for cash inflows and outflows in the cash flow from investing line item in the cash flow statement.

*Recognized Revenue*

Once a company provides the service, bookings become recognized revenue and can be recorded as accounts receivable.

*Retained Earnings*

Retained earnings are essentially a company's savings account. Any new earnings from the period are added onto previous earnings in the shareholder's equity section of the balance sheet.

*Return on Investment (ROI)*

A target multiple of the amount of cash invested in a business, typically 8-10x for early stage investors and 3-5x for late stage or growth equity investors.

*Revealed Preferences*

An economic framework that depicts consumers and producers as rational actors that make decisions in which they are better off. If a consumer chooses Airbnb over a hotel, they do so because Airbnb is cheaper or more convenient. If a driver chooses Uber over purchasing a taxi, it is likely because Uber is the more convenient option.

*Risk Factor Summation Method*

A valuation method that focuses on the overall risk profile of a company while using a broad set of factors and a median pre-revenue valuation that is region-specific.

*Runway*

The amount of venture capital that remains in a company's bank account.

*Rule of Thirds*

A straightforward rule of thumb valuation that gives pre-revenue investors a third of the company, leaving another third for founders and the remaining third for future C-level executives and management.

*Salaries Payable*

Employees earn a salary as they work, but aren't paid immediately. Before the company pays the salary of an employee, that amount of money will be accounted for under salaries payable.

*Secondary Shares*

Existing shares of stock that are sold to investors. In other words, two individuals trading shares amongst each other.

*Seed Round*

The initial round of funding for a business often composed of friends, family, angels and other early stage investors.

*Standard Value Method*

A valuation method that demarcates a pre-money valuation between $2M and $3M for pre-revenue companies no matter the business or industry. This is typically the valuation sweet spot for pre-revenue investors to achieve an 8-10x ROI upon a successful exit.

*Straight-Line Depreciation*

A standard method of depreciation where the business takes what they paid for an asset (cost of the asset) less what it would be worth at a scrap heap (salvage value) and then divide all of this by the useful life of the asset.

*Take Rate*

The proportion of gross revenue or gross transaction value (GTV) that goes directly to the company.

*Take-Private*

The act of purchasing all outstanding shares in a public company in order to return it to a privately held business entity.

*TAM (Total Addressable Market)*

Represents the market size that the new company will enter, or is currently a player.

*Terminal Value*

The extended value of the company beyond the forecasted five years in valuation techniques such as the discounted cash flow method.

*Treasury Stock*

Represents a company's own shares that they bought back from the market. Since cash is flowing out of the company to buy shares, the treasury stock is a negative account or a contra-equity account.

*Upside Scenario*

A scenario or case in which a portfolio company creates substantially good return for the venture firm. Early stage venture capital firms rely on one or two companies achieving this.

*Unicorn*

A term for technology companies valued at over $1B.

*Valuation*

Both an art and a science, valuation determines the current worth of a business.

*Valuation Divergence*

Popularized by the late angel investor, Luis Villalobos, the phenomena of a venture's value increasing and its early stage private shares increasing at a much lower rate. Early stage investors will experience a cash-on-cash ROI decrease or valuation divergence of as much as 3-5x.

*Venture Capital Method*

Determining what a firm thinks a company will be worth at exit (anticipated post-money valuation) through market conditions and industry multiples, then dividing this number by the anticipated return on investment (ROI) to arrive at a current post-money valuation. After subtracting the investment amount requested, the investor can arrive at an appropriate pre-money valuation.

*Venture Capitalists*

A group of investors who receive their money from several different sources who do not share in direct ownership of the portfolio companies. Venture capitalists invest in early- to mid-stage private companies in order to earn large returns on the investment.

*Venture Debt*

Injecting capital into an early stage business in the form of short-term loans so as not to further dilute equity that can be used for later rounds. A company may need and request venture debt to meet sales demand so equity can be saved for more substantial initiatives like national expansion.

*Warrants*

In the context of venture capital, a clause that gives investors the right to convert debt into equity in a given time frame.

*Weighted Average Cost of Capital (WACC)*

The return that equity owners and lenders expect from a company. WACC is the discount rate used in the discounted cash flow valuation method.

*Working Capital*

A company's ability to cover short-term liabilities. In order to benchmark this figure, a company takes current assets and subtracts current liabilities.

# ABOUT ME

Prior to enrolling in Columbia University, I co-founded Movement Park, a collaborative exchange platform for filmmakers. I raised a small amount of capital, established a board of advisors and ran the company for two years along with my friend, Ben Webber, who also managed the scope of the project and day-to-day web development.

I am currently an undergrad at Columbia University in the City of New York and have had the opportunity to work for some great companies. In the summer of my freshman year I worked for SRP Advisors, a buy-side M&A advisory firm where I helped middle-market private equity firms find investment opportunities for their portfolio companies through mergers and add-on acquisitions.

In the summer of my sophomore year I worked as an investment banking summer analyst at Barclays Capital in the Technology, Media and Telecommunications (TMT) group.

In my junior year at Columbia, I began working with venture firms to gain experience in the field. During that fall semester I helped build the New York base of NextGen Venture Partners, a seed-stage angel group originally based in Washington D.C., and was an Investment Fellow with DCM Ventures helping the firm analyze investment opportunities in the Greater New York Area.

I am a founder and former president of Columbia Venture Partners, a student-run analyst program that allows venture capitalists to engage students in project-based learning opportunities on a semester-to-semester basis. Most recently, I interned at Stripes Group, an NYC-based growth equity firm in the summer of 2016 and received an offer to join the team full-time in 2017.

# ACKNOWLEDGEMENTS

I just want to thank a few people that inspired me keep on pushing and pursuing a career in venture capital. I will obviously miss some people, so please forgive me in advance, if I do (P.S. these guys are all amazing people if you ever want to reach out to them).

Paul Price, Ruth Mesfun, Ian Connell, Eliot Durbin, Heather Hiles, Charles Hudson, Richard Kerby, Dan Abelon, Stephen DeBerry, Andrew Diaz, David Hall, Nicole Gervasio, Ben Webber, Mary Woldegiorgis, Christopher Jimenez y West, David Cheng, Leena Dai, Kelsey Morgan, Ripley Carroll, Madeline Brooks, Matthew Goodyear, Corey Miller, Brendan Syron, Aaron Walker, Annis Sands, Cedric Brown, John Henry, Fon Powell, Elizabeth Hou, Dan O'Flaherty, Daniela Lopez, Ryan Smith, Jewel Burks, Chike Ukaegbu, Oscar Alvarez, Haidar Jamal-Baba, Aidan Levy, Jeriel Acosta, Ariel Lopez, John Gannon, Bradley Harrison, Owen Davis, Justin Wexler, Jon Ma, Brian Aoaeh, John Azubuike, Clint Korver, Safiya Walker, Carlos José Sánchez, Carlos Henriquez, Emmanuel Valtierra, Nico Suarez, Miles Jenkins, Maleek Akeju, Serena Tsay, Sherman Julmis, Hugo Sanchez, Varun Arora, Ryan Luo, Patrick Pistor, Mac Bolak, Jon Marchetti, Jeevan Karamsetty, Indra Sofian, David Selverian, Mercedes Chien, Eric Tarczynski, Contrary Capital, Columbia Venture Partners, Columbia Organization of Rising Entrepreneurs and Stripes Group.

Thank you guys!

# ENDNOTES AND REFERENCES

[1] PricewaterhouseCoopers, San Francisco Center for Economic Development. *Venture Capital Research Report Q3 2016.* 2016.
http://sfced.org/wp-content/uploads/2016/11/VC-Report-Q3-2016.pdf

[2] Warburg Pincus. "iParadigms to be Acquired for $752 Million by Insight Venture Partners and GIC." Warburg Pincus Press Release, June 2, 2014.
http://www.warburgpincus.com/content/uploads/2015/04/iParadigms-Press-Release.pdf.

[3] Dominguez, J. and B. Bailey. "Growth Capital: Investing in Rapid Growth, High Potential Companies." SVB Capital, October 14, 2008.
http://www.svb.com/pdfs/vc_2008_oct.pdf;
Mooradian, P., A. Auerbach and M. Quealy. "U.S. Market Commentary: Growth Equity Is All Grown Up." Cambridge Associates, June 25, 2013.
http://40926u2govf9kuqen1ndit018su.wpengine.netdna-cdn.com/wp-content/uploads/2014/02/Growth-Equity-June-2013.pdf.

[4] Cheng, L. "Why Growth Equity Is The Best Risk/Reward in Private Equity." Larry Cheng Blog, July 26, 2016.
https://larrycheng.com/2010/04/17/why-growth-equity-is-the-best-riskreward-in-private-equity/.

[5] Wilson, F. "What Is A Good Venture Return?" AVC, March 20, 2009.
http://avc.com/2009/03/what-is-a-good-venture-return/;
Yang, J. "30% IRR — A Primer for First-Time Entrepreneurs." The Conscience of a VC, June 24, 2014.
http://www.jmyang.com/blog/2014/6/24/30-irr-a-primer-for-first-time-entrepreneurs;
Peters, B. "Venture Capital Funds - How the Math Works" Angel Blog, December 5, 2008.
http://www.angelblog.net/Venture_Capital_Funds_How_the_Math_Works.html.

[6] Mooradian, P., A. Auerbach and M. Quealy. "U.S. Market Commentary: Growth Equity Is All Grown Up."; "Global Buyout & Growth Equity Index and Selected Benchmark Statistics." Cambridge Associates, June 30, 2015.
http://40926u2govf9kuqen1ndit018su.wpengine.netdna-cdn.com/wp-content/uploads/2015/10/Public-Global-BO-GE-2015-Q2.pdf;
"What is Growth Equity?" Tahosa Capital (publishing data unavailable).
http://tahosacapital.com/perspective/growth-equity/.

[7] Hammond, E., J. Clark and I. King. "NXP Semiconductors to Acquire Freescale for $11.8 Billion." Bloomberg Technology, March 1, 2015. http://www.bloomberg.com/news/articles/2015-03-02/nxp-semiconductors-to-acquire-freescale-for-11-8-billion.

[8] "2015-Q4 Private Equity Trends Report." Private Equity Growth Capital Council, February, 11, 2016. http://www.investmentcouncil.org/app/uploads/2015-q4-pegcc-private-equity-trends-report.pdf.

[9] Gordan, P. "Venture Debt: A Capital Idea for Startups." Kauffman Fellows, August 24, 2012. http://www.kauffmanfellows.org/journal_posts/venture-debt-a-capital-idea-for-startups/.

[10] Ibid.

[11] Ibid.

[12] Ibid.; Chaudhary, D. "Why dilute equity, when you can have venture debt?" Forbes India, April 28, 2016. http://india.forbes.com/article/work-in-progress/why-dilute-equity-when-you-can-have-venture-debt/43043/1.

[13] Westwood, R. "How To Fund A Business With Venture Debt" Forbes, Dec 8, 2015. http://www.forbes.com/sites/ryanwestwood/2015/12/08/how-to-fund-a-business-with-venture-debt/#2e8641a04295.

[14] Franklin, N. "Presenting: The Ultimate SaaS Metrics Cheat Sheet." ChartMogul Blog, January 6, 2015. https://blog.chartmogul.com/the-ultimate-saas-metrics-cheat-sheet/#gs.Q3JWvKU.

[15] Deeter, B. "Bessemer Cloud Computing Law #5: Play Moneyball with the 5 C's." Bessemer Venture Partners Blog, October 2, 2012. https://www.bvp.com/blog/bessemer-cloud-computing-law-5-play-moneyball-5-c's;
Murphy, L. "SaaS Churn Rate: What's Acceptable?" Sixteen Ventures Blog, February 5, 2013. http://sixteenventures.com/saas-churn-rate#comments.

[16] Wilson, F. "Burn Rate." AVC, December 5, 2011. http://avc.com/2011/12/burn-rate/.

[17] Murphy, L. "SaaS Churn: Measure Revenue or Customer Retention?" SaaS Growth Strategies, July 15, 2013. http://sixteenventures.com/saas-churn-revenue-customer;
"Essential SaaS Metrics: Revenue Retention Fundamentals." SaaS Capital, November 12, 2015. http://www.saas-capital.com/blog/essential-saas-metrics-revenue-retention-fundamentals/.

[18] Murphy, L. "SaaS Churn: Measure Revenue or Customer Retention?"

[19] Kissmetrics. "How To Calculate Lifetime Value – The Infographic." Kissmetrics Blog, August 18, 2011.
https://blog.kissmetrics.com/how-to-calculate-lifetime-value/.

[20] Kissmetrics. "Customer Acquisition Cost: The One Metric That Can Determine Your Company's Fate." Kissmetrics Blog, April 22, 2015.
https://blog.kissmetrics.com/customer-acquisition-cost/.

[21] The CLV/CAC ratio is also commonly referred to as the LTV (Lifetime Value)/CAC ratio.

[22] Klipfolio. "Customer Lifetime Value to Customer Acquisition Ratio (CLV:CAC)." Klipfolio Blog (publishing data unavailable).
https://www.klipfolio.com/resources/kpi-examples/saas-metrics/customer-lifetime-value-to-customer-acquisition-ratio#gref.

[23] Cowan, D. "Bessemer Cloud Computing Law #6: Build the Revenue Engine." BVP Blog, October 2, 2012.
https://www.bvp.com/blog/bessemer-cloud-computing-law-6-build-revenue-engine;
Tunguz, T. "The Importance of Payback Period for SaaS Startups." Thomas Tunguz Blog, September 21, 2015.
http://tomtunguz.com/payback_period_cash/.

[24] Cohen, J. "Visualizing the Interactions Between CAC, Churn and LTV." A Smart Bear, February 11, 2014.
http://blog.asmartbear.com/visualizing-the-interactions-between-cac-churn-and-ltv.html.

[25] Sanwal, A. "Funding To VC-Backed Education Technology Startups Grows 503% over 5 Years." CB Insights, July 27, 2015.
https://www.cbinsights.com/blog/ed-tech-funding-on-pace-record-year/.

[26] Markets and Markets."Education Technology (Ed Tech) and Smart Classrooms Market by Hardware (IWB, Projectors, Displays, Printers), Systems (LMC, LCMS, LCDS, SRS, DMS), Technologies (Gaming, Analytics, ERP, Dashboards) - Global Forecast to 2020." Market and Markets, accessed 2016 (publishing data unavailable).
http://www.marketsandmarkets.com/Market-Reports/educational-technology-ed-tech-market-1066.html.

[27] Byrd, R. "Udemy Hires Darren Shimkus to Lead Udemy for Business Team and Meet Increasing Demand For High-Quality Corporate Training." Udemy Press, September 2, 2015.
https://press.udemy.com/udemy-hires-darren-shimkus-to-lead-udemy-for-business-team-and-meet-increasing-demand-for-high-quality-corporate-training/.

[28] Wiechers, E. "Udemy Collaborates with Leading Training Providers in Singapore to Bring Training Programs Online." Udemy Press, November 4, 2015.

https://press.udemy.com/udemy-collaborates-with-leading-training-providers-in-singapore-to-bring-training-programs-online/.

[29] McCrum, D., R. Wigglesworth and E. Moore. "Fed's Decision to Hold Rates Adds Uncertainty." Financial Times, September 25, 2015.
http://www.ft.com/cms/s/0/b65c519c-6355-11e5-97e9-7f0bf5e7177b.html;
Duggan, J. "Chinese Stock Markets Continue to Nosedive as Regulator Warns of Panic." The Guardian, July 8, 2015.
https://www.theguardian.com/business/2015/jul/08/china-stock-markets-continue-nosedive-as-regulator-warns-of-panic.

[30] "Excite@Home." Gale Encyclopedia of E-Commerce on encyclopedia.com (publishing data unavailable).
http://www.encyclopedia.com/doc/1G2-3405300181.html;
Knecht, G. "Amazon.com Files for IPO, Valuing Firm at $300 Million." The Wall Street Journal, March 25, 1997.
http://www.wsj.com/articles/SB859220492737069500;

[31] Kokalitcheva, K. "This Is the Latest $1 Billion Tech Company to IPO." Fortune, May 20, 2015.
http://fortune.com/2015/05/20/shopify-ipo-pricing/;
Picker, L. and A. Massa. "Box Opens at $20.20, IPO at $14.00." Bloomberg Technology, January 22, 2015.
http://www.bloomberg.com/news/articles/2015-01-23/box-said-to-raise-175-million-pricing-u-s-ipo-above-range;
Rao, L. and D. Primack. "Square prices IPO at just $9 per share, valued at $2.9 billion." Fortune, November 8, 2015.
http://fortune.com/2015/11/18/square-prices-ipo/.

[32] Coleman, J. "Trends in High Pre-Money Valuation Financings." The Entrepreneur Report: Private Company Financing and Trends. Wilson, Sonsini, Goodrich & Rosati (WSGR) Database, August 15, 2014
https://www.wsgr.com/publications/PDFSearch/entreport/1H2014/private-company-financing-trends.htm;
Grinda, F. "Macro Perspective: The Startup Party Is Far From Over!" Fabrice Grinda Blog, December 2, 2015.
http://www.fabricegrinda.com/entrepreneurship/macro-perspective-the-startup-party-is-far-from-over/;
Craven, S. "Unicorns, Thoroughbreds and Work Horses." Sand Hill Global Advisors, August 10, 2016.
http://www.sandhillglobaladvisors.com/blog/unicorns-thoroughbreds-and-work-horses.

[33] Torenberg, E. "Episode 59: Sarah Tavel." Audio blog post. Maker Stories. Product Hunt, January 25, 2016.
https://www.producthunt.com/podcasts/product-hunt-maker-stories-sarah-tavel.

[34] "What Is the Difference Between EBIT and Operating Income?" Investopedia, January 20, 2015.

http://www.investopedia.com/ask/answers/012015/what-difference-between-ebit-and-operating-income.asp.

[35] Pomerleau, K. "Corporate Income Tax Rates Around the World, 2014." Tax Foundation, August 27, 2014.
http://taxfoundation.org/sites/default/files/docs/FF436_0.pdf

[36] Campbell P. "A Comprehensive Guide to SaaS Finance (Bookings vs. Revenue vs. Collections vs. MRR)." Profitwell Blog, September 30, 2015.
http://blog.profitwell.com/understanding-saas-accounting-saas-bookings-saas -revenue-saas-collections.

[37] Wilson, F. "Bookings vs Revenues vs Collections." AVC, August 16, 2010.
http://avc.com/2010/08/bookings-vs-revenues-vs-collections/.

[38] Fernandes, J. "IRR Analysis: Years Invested vs. Return Multiple." One Match Ventures Blog, July 6, 2013.
http://onematchventures.com/irr-analysis-years-invested-vs-return-multiple/;
Wilson, F. "What Is A Good Venture Return?"

[39] "What's the Difference Between Pre-Money and Post-Money?" Investopedia, July 5, 2007.
http://www.investopedia.com/ask/answers/114.asp.

[40] McClure, B. "DCF Analysis: Coming Up With A Fair Value." Investopedia, January 25, 2006.
http://www.investopedia.com/university/dcf/dcf4.asp;
"Terminal Value." Macabacus, May 28, 2009.
http://macabacus.com/valuation/dcf/terminal-value.

[41] Damodaran, A. "Valuing Young, Start-up and Growth Companies: Estimation Issues and Valuation Challenges." Stern School of Business, New York University, May 2009.
http://people.stern.nyu.edu/adamodar/pdfiles/papers/younggrowth.pdf.

[42] Black, F. and M. Scholes. "The Pricing of Options and Corporate Liabilities." The Journal of Political Economy, Vol. 81, No. 3 (May - Jun., 1973), p. 637-654.

[43] Sahlman, W. and D. Scherlis. "A Method For Valuing High-Risk, Long-Term Investments: The Venture Capital Method." Harvard Business School Background Note 288-006, July 1987. (Revised October 2009).

[44] For in-depth examples visit vcmethod.com.

[45] Berkery Noyes. "An Overview of M&A in the Healthcare/Pharma Information and Technology Industry." Berkery Noyes Press Release, April 10, 2016.
http://www.berkerynoyes.com/publication/pr/HCWhitePaperQ12014.aspx.

[46] Sohl, J. "The Angel Investor Market in 2015: A Buyers' Market." Center for Venture Research, May 25, 2015.
https://paulcollege.unh.edu/sites/paulcollege.unh.edu/files/webform/Full%20 Year%202015%20Analysis%20Report.pdf.

[47] Villalobos, L. "Valuation Divergence." Kauffman Foundation eVenturing Collection: Valuing Pre-Revenue Companies, July 7, 2007.
https://www.angelcapitalassociation.org/data/Documents/Resources/AngelCapitalEducation/ACEF_-_Valuing_Pre-revenue_Companies.pdf.

[48] Suster, M. "Mark Suster: The Authoritative Guide to Pro-Rata Rights." Inc. Magazine, October 13, 2014.
http://www.inc.com/mark-suster/the-authoritative-guide-to-prorata-rights.html.

[49] Villalobos, L. "Investment Valuations of Seed and Early Stage Ventures." Kauffman Foundation eVenturing Collection: Valuing Pre-Revenue Companies, July 7, 2007.
https://www.angelcapitalassociation.org/data/Documents/Resources/AngelCapitalEducation/ACEF_-_Valuing_Pre-revenue_Companies.pdf.

[50] VT Knowledgeworks. "Valuation Models for Pre-Revenue Companies." VT Knowledgeworks, Accessed 2016 (publishing data unavailable).
http://vtknowledgeworks.com/sites/all/themes/vtknowledgeworks/files/Valuation_Models_for_Pre-Revenue_Companies.pdf.

[51] Amis, D. Winning Angels: The 7 Fundamentals of Early Stage Investing. New Jersey: FT Press, 2001; Berkus, D. Extending the Runway. Los Angeles: Berkus Press, 2004; Berkus, D. Berkonomics. Los Angeles: Berkus Press, 2011.

[52] Payne, B. "Current Pre-Money Valuations of Pre-Revenue Companies." Bill Payne & Associates, April 11, 2011.
http://billpayne.com/2011/04/11/current-pre-money-valuations-of-pre-revenue-companies.html.

[53] Sohl, J. "The Angel Investor Market in 2015: A Buyers' Market."

[54] Mothersill, W., Watson, B. et al. Age of the Angel: Best Practices for Angel Groups and Investors. National Angel Capital Organization, January 29, 2009.

[55] Notable iterations of some of these valuation methods include the score-card method, Cayenne Consulting method and the Bill Payne method.

[56] Gurley, B. "All Markets Are Not Created Equal: 10 Factors To Consider When Evaluating Digital Marketplaces." Above the Crowd, November 13, 2012.
http://abovethecrowd.com/2012/11/13/all-markets-are-not-created-equal-10-factors-to-consider-when-evaluating-digital-marketplaces/.

[57] "2016 National Undergraduate Venture Cup." Virginia Venture Fund, April 13, 2016.
http://www.virginiaventurefund.com/2016-national-venture-cup/.

[58] Brooks, Madeline. Personal Interview. November 5, 2016.

[59] Carroll, Ripley. Personal Interview. April 6, 2016.

[60] Enright, Nicholas. Personal Interview. March 31, 2016.

[61] Wexler, Justin. Personal Interview. April, 6, 2016.

[62] Greer, Brandon. Personal Interview. April 1, 2016.

[63] Shein, Jason. Personal Interview. March, 28 2016.

Made in the USA
Columbia, SC
23 December 2017